The Value of ESG Metrics in the Investment Process

Alexander Schleipfer

The Value of ESG Metrics in the Investment Process

Leveraging ESG Metrics in the Construction of European Stock Portfolios

Springer Gabler

Alexander Schleipfer
Mergers and Acquisitions
HHL Leipzig Graduate School of Management
Leipzig, Germany

Leipzig (Germany), HHL Leipzig Graduate School of Management, Dissertation, 2024

ISBN 978-3-658-49788-0 ISBN 978-3-658-49789-7 (eBook)
https://doi.org/10.1007/978-3-658-49789-7

This Springer Gabler imprint is published by the registered company Springer Fachmedien Wiesbaden GmbH, part of Springer Nature.
The registered company address is: Abraham-Lincoln-Str. 46, 65189 Wiesbaden, Germany

To my mother, Erika, and my father, Lothar.

Foreword

As a Partner of Deloitte Germany's strategy consultancy, I have gained over 20 years of experience in the finance industry, with stints in asset management units of HSBC and BayernLB. Additionally, I am a constituent member of the German Government's Sustainable Finance Advisory Board. This board was founded to develop Germany into one of the leading sustainable finance locations.

Working with institutional investors and corporates on their sustainability and transition strategies, I assist clients in building the path from compliance and reporting by growing business opportunities aligned with carbon neutrality, converting regulatory and corporate goals and ambitions into potential. While any strategic decision requires facts and figures, it is needless to underpin that the internalization of externalities in these facts and figures is the necessary complex challenge of our century. The dissertation *ESG Investing—At the Cost of Return?* therefore marks a significant step. It evaluates the link between ESG metrics and financial returns, offering insights through rigorous data analysis and introducing the ESG-F framework, which provides an actionable approach to integrating these metrics into an investment decision process. Investors and regulators equally enjoy transparency on data, formula and metrics. The work's deep dive is therefore a masterpiece for stakeholders, providing a practical tool for more transparency, leading to a profound judgment and a portfolio construction that offers far more long-term understanding.

Sustainable finance regulation aimed high in Europe in the last years, now facing pushbacks on ambition level and acceptance in practicability. We, as investors, regulators, and the asset management industry, need to focus to ensure the short-term credibility for our long-term goals. This dissertation provides precisely that focus, offering a hands-on, research-based perspective on ESG investing that strengthens both immediate actions and sustainable finance aspirations for the future.

Wiebke Merbeth
Constituent Member
Sustainable Finance Advisory Committee
of the German Federal Government
Partner, Deloitte Monitor, Germany

Author's Preface

> *Economic performance is the first responsibility of a business. A business that does not show a profit at least equal to its cost of capital is socially irresponsible, as it wastes society's resources [...]. But economic performance is not the sole responsibility of a business. Power must always be balanced by responsibility.*
>
> *– Peter F. Drucker, 1993, p. 92.*

Peter Drucker's vision of corporate social responsibility outlined in *The Post-Capitalist Society* has often come to mind during the years I have spent on completing this dissertation. As a pioneer of modern management, Drucker framed corporate social responsibility not only as an ethical duty but as a strategic advantage. He truly believed that corporate social responsibility was not just a moral obligation but also a strategic advantage. Businesses should strive to do well by doing good, blending social and economic goals. Where the invisible hand of markets does not suffice, the visible hand, in form of regulations, becomes necessary. In this context, accounting rules for environmental, social, and governance (ESG) metrics will improve data quality, enabling asset managers to better evaluate how companies perform against these criteria and allow them to follow an ESG investing approach. Yet a key question remains: Does this pay off?

My research titled *ESG Investing—At the Cost of Return? Leveraging ESG Metrics in the Construction of European Stock Portfolios* investigates this question at the intersection of financial returns and sustainability, seeking to understand the extent to which ESG metrics can be effectively integrated into the asset management process.

Throughout my doctoral program, I have had the privilege of consulting and collaborating with companies to navigate sustainability regulations and ESG strategies. Additionally, my time spent with some of the world's largest asset managers has fueled my academic curiosity and allowed me to dive into the practical implications of ESG investing. These experiences have offered invaluable lessons learned, helping me bridge the gap between theory and practice and forming the foundation of this very dissertation.

Ultimately, this research will contribute to both academic discourse and practical applications in sustainable finance, providing researchers, professionals, and policymakers with a framework for navigating the increasing importance of ESG metrics in asset management.

Thank you to every single one of you who has supported my research journey. I extend my deepest gratitude to Wiebke Merbeth, Partner at Monitor Deloitte and Constituent Member of the German Government's Sustainable Finance Advisory Board, and Anne Simpson, Global Head of Sustainability at Franklin Templeton Investments and Lecturer at Berkeley Haas, for their invaluable insights into sustainable finance, asset management, and global regulations. I am especially grateful to my supervisor Alexander Lahmann, Chair of Mergers and Acquisitions at HHL Leipzig Graduate School of Management, for his unwavering support, as well as to the academic communities of HHL and Berkeley Haas for their intellectual inspiration.

Leipzig
August 2024

Alexander Schleipfer

Contents

Abbreviations

AUM	Assets Under Management
CDP	Carbon Disclosure Project
EBSCO	Business Source Premier
EFRAG	European Financial Reporting Advisory Group
ESG	Environmental, Social and Governance
ESM	Electronic Supplementary Material
ETF	Exchange-Traded Fund
EVIC	Enterprise Value Including Cash
GHG	Greenhouse Gas
ICB	Industry Classification Benchmark
ICC	Intraclass Correlation Coefficient
IFRS	International Financial Reporting Standards
ISS	Institutional Shareholder Services
ISSB	International Sustainability Standards Board
KPI	Key Performance Indicator
M&A	Mergers and Acquisitions
NSRI	Non-Socially Responsible Investing
NZIA	Net-Zero Insurance Alliance
SDG	Sustainable Development Goal
SFDR	Sustainable Finance Disclosure Regulation
SLR	Systematic Literature Review
SPAR-4-SLR	Scientific Procedures and Rationales for Systematic Literature Reviews
SRI	Socially Responsible Investing
TCFD	Task Force on Climate-Related Financial Disclosures
UN PRI	UN Principles for Responsible Investment
UNEP FI	United Nations Environment Programme Finance Initiative
WoS	Web of Science

List of Figures

List of Tables

1 Introduction and Statement

In recent years, capital market activity has been frenzied, with low interest rates, extensive fiscal support during the COVID-19 pandemic, and a resounding call for investors and asset managers to consider environmental, social, and governance (ESG) factors. However, as the macroeconomic environment has tightened, production and product prices have risen, and more critical debates on ESG investing have emerged. While some argue that this investment strategy drives up costs, contributes to higher prices, and diminishes investment returns, others maintain that incorporating ESG factors enhances investment returns.

The most relevant reference in the context of ESG investing is probably "Larry Fink's 2021 letter to CEOs," in which the CEO of the world's largest asset management company, BlackRock Inc, notes that "companies with better ESG profiles are performing better than their peers." Another relevant quote is that from the former president of the European Commission, Jean-Claude Juncker, during his keynote speech at a 2018 conference on financing sustainable growth: "Sustainability should not be seen as a niche within the financial system. It must define our financial system. And it is an opportunity we must grasp before others do" (European Commission, 2018).

The old idiom that one should "put one's money where one's mouth is" may lead investors to put their money into companies that follow their values and act in an environmentally friendly manner to reduce their environmental footprint and that take social responsibility and pursue fairness in their governance practices. The fact that capital has power that investors exercise through their investment decisions has been vividly illustrated, not least by phenomena such as

A. Schleipfer, *The Value of ESG Metrics in the Investment Process*, https://doi.org/10.1007/978-3-658-49789-7_1

WallStreetBets.[1] ESG investing is thus fostered by regulatory and demand-side factors.

1.1 Regulatory Context

Various ESG reporting standards have been developed globally. Some of the most significant, on a worldwide scale, are the following: The International Sustainability Standards Board (ISSB), which was established in November 2021 by the International Financial Reporting Standards (IFRS) Foundation, has issued IFRS S1 and S2, which can be adopted by individual states. On March 6, 2024, the United States Securities and Exchange Commission finalized a rule, that will initially be mandatory for large listed entities that are considered "accelerated filers." The European Financial Reporting Advisory Group (EFRAG) has launched a directive on corporate sustainability reporting that introduces clearly defined standards: the European Sustainability Reporting Standards.[2]

The ESG regulatory initiatives taken by the European Union (EU) and its member states are aligned with the European Green Deal, which aims to make Europe the first climate-neutral continent by 2050. These initiatives are designed to make ESG matters more approachable for institutional and retail investors, unlocking additional investments to finance the transition to a more sustainable and inclusive economy. A key element of the Green Deal is the European Green Deal Investment Plan, which aims to unlock at least EUR 1 trillion in sustainable investment by 2030 to support the transition to climate neutrality. The EU's associated strategy for sustainable finance is implemented through a set of ESG guidelines and regulations that have significant implications for financial system

[1] WallStreetBets refers to an online community of retail investors on Reddit. The community gained prominence during the 2021 GameStop (GME) short squeeze, where coordinated retail trading significantly impacted stock prices, challenging institutional investors. This event exemplified how collective retail action can influence market outcomes, analogous to how ESG investors mobilize capital to influence corporate behavior in line with their environmental, social, and governance values.

[2] EFRAG has already submitted a draft for cross-sectoral standards on behalf of the EU Commission. This draft includes two generally applicable European Sustainability Reporting Standards (ESRS 1 and ESRS 2), five in the environmental area (ESRS E1–E5), four in the social area (ESRS S1–S4), and one in the area of corporate governance (ESRS G1). There are 12 standards with 82 disclosure requirements across 117 sustainability topics (topics, sub-topics, sub-sub-topics) with over 1,000 data points. The materiality analysis reduces this to sector- and company-relevant criteria. In parallel, EFRAG will develop sector-specific standards by the end of June 2026 (EFRAG, 2023a, 2023b; European Council, 2024).

participants, particularly in areas related to the collection and reporting of data on ESG issues.

In 2022, the global assets of insurance companies amounted to approximately USD 35.6 trillion, with a further USD 40.9 trillion in assets held by pension funds (Financial Stability Board, 2023). The total assets under management (AUM) amounted to USD 98.3 trillion, exceeding the global GDP of approximately USD 96 trillion (BCG, 2023; International Monetary Fund, 2024; Opimas, 2022). Achieving the environmental goal of net zero by 2050 requires over USD 7 trillion per annum under current financing conditions. This funding gap can only be addressed through the power of the financial system (Deloitte, 2023).

Regulatory authorities, such as the EU, have implemented regulations including investment-related ESG reporting requirements that apply to asset owners, investment managers, and service providers. Regulators expect institutions to consider ESG risks in their scenario analyses and stress tests and to take advantage of relevant investment opportunities. In this context, the EU is a high-regulation jurisdiction (see Table 1.1). France can be considered separately, as its ESG reporting obligations reflect and are in some respects stricter than the EU obligations.

The centerpiece of the EU ESG reporting framework is the Sustainable Finance Disclosure Regulation (SFDR), which mandates that asset owners and investment managers provide investment-related reporting at the company and product levels (European Parliament & Council of the European Union, 2019). The SFDR regulates how sustainability risks are disclosed and integrated into investment decisions and how the adverse sustainability impacts of products should be assessed.

Table 1.1 Jurisdictions by Investment-Related ESG Reporting Requirements. (Note: From Woods et al., 2022)

Jurisdiction	Regions and Countries
High regulation	EU, France, Hong Kong, UK
Medium regulation	Australia, China, Japan
Low regulation	Canada, US

The SFDR complements existing EU ESG reporting frameworks, including the pan-European Personal Pension Product, the revised directive on institutions for occupational retirement provision (IORP II), and the regulation on packaged retail and insurance-based investment products. The amended Shareholder Rights Directive (SRD II) imposes obligations on asset owners and asset managers to integrate stewardship into their strategies and disclose their proxy voting practices (European Parliament & Council of the European Union, 2019).

Asset owners and managers must also disclose how their activities align with the mandates for environmentally sustainable economic activity under the EU's Taxonomy Regulation. Investment managers must report on various aspects of their investment activities including the long-term performance related to environmentally sustainable economic activities, as required by the EU's Taxonomy Regulation. Additionally, while not explicitly mandated by the Taxonomy, they are encouraged to include disclosures on social outcomes and engagement as part of their broader ESG reporting practices. Despite the comprehensive nature of these regulations, there is currently no EU-wide obligation for investment organizations to report in accordance with the recommendations of the Task Force on Climate-Related Financial Disclosures (TCFD); however, states such as France and the United Kingdom (UK) have instituted such requirements (TCFD, 2017). These regulations are designed to improve investors' risk management and prevent greenwashing through enhanced transparency, which, in turn, builds trust in responsible investing and can support efforts to fill the present annual USD 7 trillion funding gap to reach net zero.

At the company level, a government's introduction of new or stricter ESG regulations may influence business models. From an investor's perspective, this could threaten company profitability, necessitating investment in compliance, or serve as a competitive advantage for those already operating within the proposed regulatory bounds. According to MSCI, there is a correlation between the ESG ratings it assigns to companies and the cost of capital; companies with higher MSCI ESG ratings tend to face lower capital costs than those with lower ratings (Lodh, 2020). This correlation was also confirmed by Priem & Gabellone (2022) using STOXX Europe 600 and Refinitiv ESG score data.[3]

1.2 Demand for ESG Investments

Analyzing the fund market is a way to assess the demand side of ESG investing and ascertain whether "sustainable investing" (often seen as synonymous with ESG investing) represents merely a niche in the financial market or a significant

[3] If the ESG profile of a company significantly impacts its access to capital, ESG criteria may gain more weight in mergers and acquisitions (M&A) activities, such as due diligence, and may become a decisive factor in M&A decisions. Additionally, companies may actively work to improve their ESG scores or ratings to benefit from lower capital costs. This could lead to a higher market valuation, an outcome that will be examined in the course of this study.

trend. According to Morgan Stanley, in December 2023 the AUM of sustainable funds[4] accounted for USD 3.4 trillion, equal to 7.2% of the fund's total global AUM; this percentage grew annually before 2023 (see Fig. 1.1). This statistic indicates that ESG investing is far from being a niche area, especially in Europe, where 87% of global sustainable funds are based at the end of 2023 (10% in North and South America and 3% in all other regions).

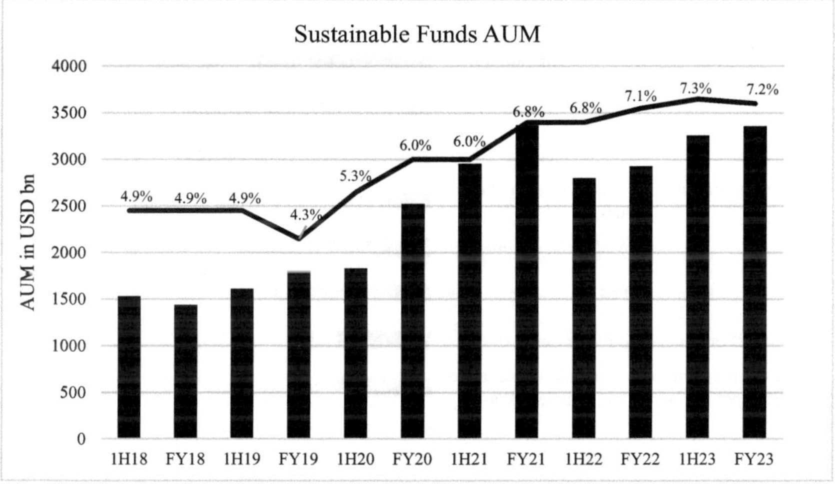

Fig. 1.1 Sustainable Funds AUM Between 2018 and 2023. (Note: Adapted from Morgan Stanley Institute for Sustainable Investing, 2024)

Morningstar reported a slowdown in international inflows to sustainable funds in 2023, with US investors withdrawing USD 13 billion in a backlash against ESG principles (Bioy et al., 2024).

Besides the existing demand for ESG investing, another potential driver of interest in ESG is the greater transparency resulting from the introduced regulations, which mitigate ESG risks by integrating them into the investment process. The critical question here is whether this approach changes the risk–return ratio in an unfavorable direction. That is, does integrating ESG considerations lead to

[4] Morgan Stanley uses the terms "ESG funds" and "sustainable funds" synonymously, which is common practice.

a situation where the reduction in risk is outweighed by the sacrifice in returns, ultimately reducing returns? According to a survey by Cerulli Associates—a leading research and consulting firm in the asset management industry—and Russell Investments (2021), risk mitigation and client demand are the largest drivers of ESG investing (Fig. 1.2).

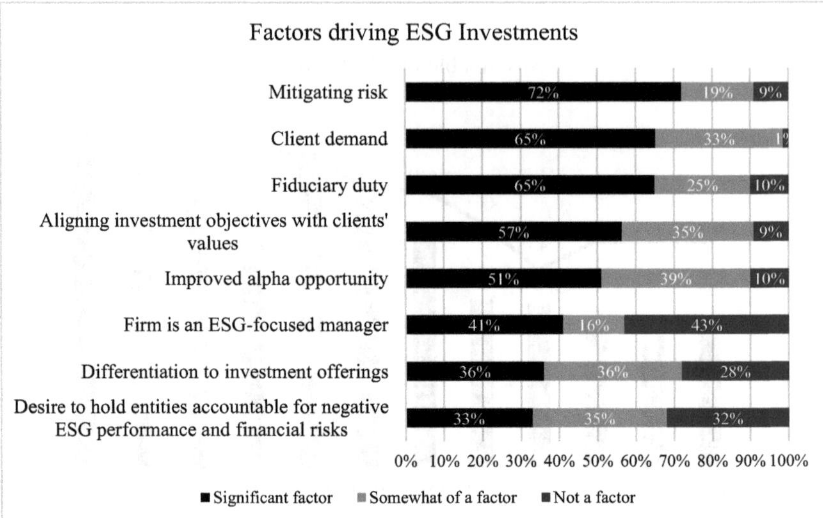

Fig. 1.2 Factors Driving ESG Investment According to Ten World-Leading Asset Managers. (Note: Adapted from Cerulli Associates and Russell Investments, 2021)

Morgan Stanley's Institute for Sustainable Investing supports these findings, indicating that while there is a demand from private investors to invest in companies whose values align with their own, risk mitigation remains critical when incorporating ESG criteria according to asset managers (2019). This is particularly true for insurance and pension funds, which are considered long-term investors interested in the mitigation of risk. In Europe, the insurance industry is the largest institutional investor. Its core business model involves receiving premiums from policyholders, which are then invested to fulfill future claims and benefits. While some claims may arise within a year, others, particularly those related to savings and pension products, may extend over decades (Insurance

Europe, 2021; Luxembourg for Finance, 2021). The long-term orientation inherent in the business model of insurers makes the long-term financial performance of assets important. Again, this raises the question about the impact on the risk–return ratio; incorporating ESG metrics may produce different results compared to relying solely on traditional, purely financial metrics.

Investors can also use voting rights to pressure companies to transform their business models to achieve net-zero targets. The threat of climate change and the accompanying environmental catastrophes and social challenges it brings are long-term risks to insurance companies. These risks may be especially relevant for emerging and developing economies, given their low insurance coverage; increasing wealth may also be the best chance insurance companies have to grow. Besides participating in the Net-Zero Asset Owner Alliance (NZAOA)[5], which commits members to transition their investment portfolios to net-zero greenhouse gas (GHG) emissions by 2050, many insurers are taking further action. In 2021, eight insurance companies—including industry heavyweights AXA SE, Allianz SE, Generali, Aviva plc, and Munich RE—established the Net-Zero Insurance Alliance (NZIA). The main commitments of its members are to achieve net-zero emissions across their insurance and reinsurance underwriting portfolios by 2050 (UNEP FI, 2021). At its peak, the UN-backed alliance had more than 30 member companies; this shrunk to 11 by the end of 2023 with the withdrawal of AXA SE, Allianz SE, and Munich Re (UNEP FI, 2024a; Wilkes et al., 2023).[6]

[5] The NZAOA is a United Nations-convened group of institutional investors committed to transitioning their investment portfolios to net-zero GHG emissions by 2050 in alignment with the Paris Agreement goal of limiting global warming to 1.5°C above pre-industrial levels. Founded in 2019, the alliance comprises pension funds, insurance companies, and other asset owners representing over USD 5 trillion in AUM. Members pledge to set intermediate targets every five years and to report on their progress annually, promoting accountability and transparency in their journey toward net-zero emissions (UNEP FI, n.d.).

[6] In addition to the demand for sustainable investing, if regarded from a corporate perspective, there is demand from customers, which might result in a competitive advantage and thus produce financial returns. Meier et al. (2022) investigated US-based barcode-level sales data from 2008 to 2016 and compared the sales volume of similar products in assessing MSCI E&S Rating performance of their brand owners. The findings indicate a positive correlation between a brand owner's E&S performance and local product sales and show the sales turnover declines after the publication of negative E&S news. The question is whether this also applies to other industries and if doing good comes with a higher cost structure.

1.3 Debate About ESG Investing and Research Objective

Like other companies that have withdrawn from the NZIA, the three industry heavyweights announced that they would stick to the targets of reaching net zero by 2050. It is likely that political resistance in the US and legal concerns motivated their decision to leave. Twelve companies left within two months after a letter signed by representatives of 23 Republican-led US states to NZIA on May 15, 2023, demanding information about the insurers' membership and threatening legal action for anti-competitive behavior that drives up prices (Tommy Wilkes, 2023). In April 2024, NZIA was quietly discontinued with a successor, the Forum for Insurance Transition to Net Zero (FIT), announced in April 2024 (UNEP FI, 2024b).[7]

Larry Fink may also have altered his strategy. In his 2023 annual chairman's letter to investors, he did not even mention ESG, whereas, in his 2021 letter, he wrote that BlackRock had seen how "purposeful companies with better environmental, social, and governance … profiles, have outperformed their peers" (Fink, 2021; Foster, 2023). Fink later admitted that he has ceased using the "weaponized" term ESG, as it had become excessively politicized in certain parts of the Western world, particularly in the US (Binnie, 2023). Energy crises and high inflation in 2022 have accelerated the anti-ESG movement, fueled by politicians and private investors concerned about the financial returns on their investments—these efforts have specifically focused on BlackRock. Among others, the states of Florida and Louisiana withdrew money from BlackRock funds (Brush, 2022; Kerber, 2022).

This move might be motivated by short-term political ambitions and may neglect the long-term investment performance that insurance companies and pension funds have to achieve and the long-term outperformance aimed for by BlackRock and other asset managers. One aspect of the backlash is the potentially worsened risk–return profile when comparing ESG and traditional investment approaches.

Given recent demand-side and regulatory developments, along with increased transparency and the potentially varying risk–return ratio, I investigate the impact on returns associated with incorporating ESG metrics in portfolio construction.

---

[7] UNEP FI claims to have created FIT based on the NZIA experience and takes proactive measures to address potential legal challenges concerning antitrust implications. In contrast to NZIA, which was primarily focused on the (re)insurance industry, FIT is a multistakeholder forum with diverse stakeholders, incorporating input from regulators, academic and civil society organizations, and (re)insurers (UNEP FI, 2024b).

This research is structured as follows. In Chap. 2, Section 2.1 defines the ESG investor and explores the characteristics of ESG investing. Section 2.2 provides a systematic literature review (SLR) with a focus on the current state of research on ESG investing and financial returns on the stock market. In the next Sect. 2.3, I compare popular ESG scoring and rating models. Building on this analysis, in sect. 2.4, I formulate hypotheses based on the aim of this study, which seeks to investigate whether incorporating ESG characteristics into investment approaches restricts investors' investment returns.

Chapter 3 presents empirical analyses to test the hypotheses developed in Sect. 2.4. In these analyses, ESG data are used to construct portfolios that aim to achieve competitive financial returns, with a focus on the European stock market. In Sect. 3.4, the application of the research findings is explored.

Chapter 4 synthesizes the research findings and introduces the ESG-F model, developed in light of these results. This model constitutes a comprehensive framework for ESG investors, providing practical guidance on the effective integration of ESG considerations into investment strategies.

2 Theoretical Background and Hypothesis Development

2.1 Historical and Terminological Analysis of ESG Investing

There is no agreed-upon definition of ESG investing.[1] However, there are many terms used in the literature connected to the idea of "socially responsible investing" (SRI), including "ethical investing," "green investing," and "ESG investing." In the following two subsections, I consider how ESG investing is understood in the literature and how it can be distinguished from other concepts. This analysis sets out how terms are interpreted in this dissertation and is the basis of a typological analysis of ESG investors.

2.1.1 ESG Investing Terminology

The idea of integrating socially responsible factors into investment decisions can be traced back to the 18th century when the founder of the Methodist Church, John Wesley, concluded that the use of money is the second most important principle of the New Testament (Christian History Institute, 2024; Wesley, 2024). The Methodist Church began avoiding investments in companies manufacturing

[1] For example, while Forbes characterizes "ESG investing" as investments in companies aiming to improve the world, MSCI and Deutsche Bank define it as the integration of ESG factors within financial considerations in the investment decision-making-process (Deutsche Bank AG, 2024a; MSCI, 2024; Napoletano & Katzeff, 2024).

Supplementary Information The online version contains supplementary material available at https://doi.org/10.1007/978-3-658-49789-7_2.

A. Schleipfer, *The Value of ESG Metrics in the Investment Process*, https://doi.org/10.1007/978-3-658-49789-7_2

tobacco products and liquor or promoting gambling on ethical grounds. In 1928, an ecclesiastical group in Boston established the first public offering of a fund that excluded investments in "sin industries." Stocks of this type are still commonly referred to as "sin stocks" and have become part of the more recently evolved concepts of SRI and ESG investing.

During the 1960s and 1970s, the US war in Vietnam became more and more critically regarded by the general public in North America, including by religious investors, who questioned portfolio profits associated with companies involved in war efforts. Students and young people urged institutional investors to divest from shares of Dow Chemical, which produced napalm. Agent Orange, another highly controversial chemical used during the Vietnam War, brought attention to the negative impacts of certain industries and sparked a movement toward SRI (Chomsky, 1993; Markowitz, 2012; Schueth, 2003). This agent of "herbicidal warfare," created for the US Department of Defense by Dow Chemical and Monsanto, was applied to over 1.3 million hectares of forest in South Vietnam, which accounted for 12% of its total area. This deliberate strategy to eliminate forests and crops was intended to deny cover and food to the Viet Cong (Stellman et al., 2003; Westing, 1983).

The use of Agent Orange caused significant environmental damage and health issues and raised moral concerns, prompting some to seek alternative investments that aligned with their values. The Pax World Balanced Fund, founded in 1971 by Methodist clergy, aimed to provide an investment option for those looking to avoid investing in companies that supported the Vietnam War (Broadhurst et al., 2003; Renneboog et al., 2008a).

The emergence of the First Spectrum Fund in 1971 represented an early embodiment of SRI practices, and its cofounders Thomas N. Delany and Royce N. Flippin Jr. emphasized the evaluation of companies' performance in "the environment, civil rights, and the protection of consumers" prior to investment decisions (Moscowitz, 1973, p. 15). In 1972, the Dreyfus Third Century Fund was formed with strong support from influential figures such as the presidents of the League of Women Voters and the Rockefeller Foundation, as well as a Nobel Prize winner. In its prospectus, the fund's focus was expressed as investing in companies that "show evidence in the conduct of their business, relative to other companies in the same industry or industries, of contributing to the enhancement of quality of life in America" (Moscowitz, 1973, p. 15).

Another significant milestone in the evolution of SRI and ESG investing was its important role in ending apartheid in South Africa. In 1975, Reverend Leon H. Sullivan, former pastor of the Zion Baptist Church and member of the Board of Directors of General Motors Corp., created an ethical framework for businesses operating in South Africa under apartheid. This framework, referred to as the Sullivan Principles, encouraged companies to uphold fair employment practices regardless of race and to actively strive to improve living conditions for groups that were not of European descent. The Sullivan Principles became a focal point for the growing movement against apartheid and pressured US companies to implement anti-apartheid practices (Stewart, 2011). The initiative also led to the US disinvestment movement in the 1980s, prompting anti-apartheid activists to advocate for university endowments and public pension funds to divest from companies that did not uphold certain principles (Clark & Bogran, 1999; Knight, 1990). Simultaneously in Europe, UK banks, particularly Barclays Bank, which played a central role in South Africa's financial system, faced increasing pressure to divest. This pressure came as trade unions, charitable institutions, and multiple universities withdrew their funds (Kaempfer et al., 1987; Sparkes, 2002). The European Economic Community also imposed a comprehensive embargo on trade and investment with South Africa in 1986 (Clark & Bogran, 1999).

In the literature, the idea of SRI can be traced back to Simon et al.'s (1972) use of the term "ethical investing" to describe SRI as distinct from conventional investing activity. Domini and Kinder (1984) discuss SRI in their book *Ethical investing*; the practice caught on after groups advocated for pension funds to fulfill their obligation to invest their capital in a socially responsible manner (Ferris & Rykaczewski, 1986). The authors pointed out the challenges and opportunities presented by SRI in the field of portfolio management, although, in subsequent years, the research focused on key factors for successful SRI (Diltz, 1995). In 1990, the Domini 400 Social Index was launched as the first capitalization-weighted index mutual fund based on the established screen-out of "sin stocks" of nuclear energy and weapons manufacturers, while also incorporating a best-in-class approach (Lydenberg, 2020).

The practice of refraining from investing in certain industries based on ethical criteria remains a core element of today's socially responsible and ESG investing but can also be seen as generally responsible investing. The awareness of sustainability and environmental protection increased in the 1990s and became a focus of research (Heinkel et al., 2001). Richardson and Cragg (2010) argue that SRI investors have ethical responsibilities that, in their view, moderate investment returns through corporate responsibility. To this end, they seek to practice ethical influence on the companies in which they are invested.

In 2006, the UN launched the Principles for Responsible Investment, an investor initiative where signatories commit to incorporating ESG criteria into the investment process. This followed the first mainstream mention of ESG in the UN's 2004 report *Who Cares Wins*. The 17 Sustainable Development Goals

(SDGs) adopted in 2015, as well as further regulations that have been introduced, have prompted research on "ESG investing" as well as "impact investing." As discussed in the next chapter, impact investing is mostly treated as a variant of ESG investing. Taking ESG criteria into account in the investment decision is a constant in the literature dealing with this topic, although there is no consensus definition of "ESG investing" and its closely related terms.

In the world of finance, other popular terms are used in this area, including "sustainable finance," "green finance," and "climate finance." Sustainable finance encompasses the three dimensions of ESG by considering the impact of all financial activities on the environment, society, and corporate governance practices, and on overall economic sustainability. Hence, ESG investing is a part of sustainable finance. Green finance, by contrast, focuses on environmental criteria. It specifically targets financial initiatives and investments that support environmental objectives, such as mitigating climate change, conserving natural resources, and promoting clean energy. Green finance does not include the social and governance dimensions of sustainable finance. Over the past decade, green finance has gained significant recognition, driven by the establishment of numerous national green investment banks and the rapid expansion of the green bond market. Climate finance is another specific subset of green finance. It refers to financial flows and investments that seek to support mitigation and adaptation actions to address climate change (United Nations Framework Convention on Climate Change, 2023).

The existence of SRI stocks implies that there are also stocks outside of this category. In this research, investment in these stocks is referred to as non-socially responsible investing (NSRI). NSRI stocks can be identified by examining the exclusion criteria used by asset managers and owners. For example, Eurosif (2018) surveyed 263 asset managers and owners with a combined AUM of EUR 20 trillion to identify the most commonly excluded sectors (see Fig. 2.1). According to the *Global Sustainable Investment Review 2022* by the Global Sustainable Investment Alliance, excluding particular sectors is common (see Fig. 2.2).

The Eurosif survey revealed that the primary exclusions in ESG investing were the categories controversial weapons, tobacco, and all weapons. To further examine this approach, I analyzed 10 popular SRI and ESG indices, focusing on their exclusionary sectors and characteristic screens (see Appendix A (ESM), Table A1). Each of the analyzed indices shares the practice of excluding companies that violate the 10 principles of the United Nations Global Compact,[2]

[2] The simple non-signatory of the United Nations Global Compact is not an exclusion criterion. This might be due to the fact that membership is more of a recurring annual obligation.

Fig. 2.1 Top Exclusions for European Asset Managers and Owners in 2018. (Note: GMO = Genetically Modified Organisms. Adapted from Eurosif, 2018. Own illustration)

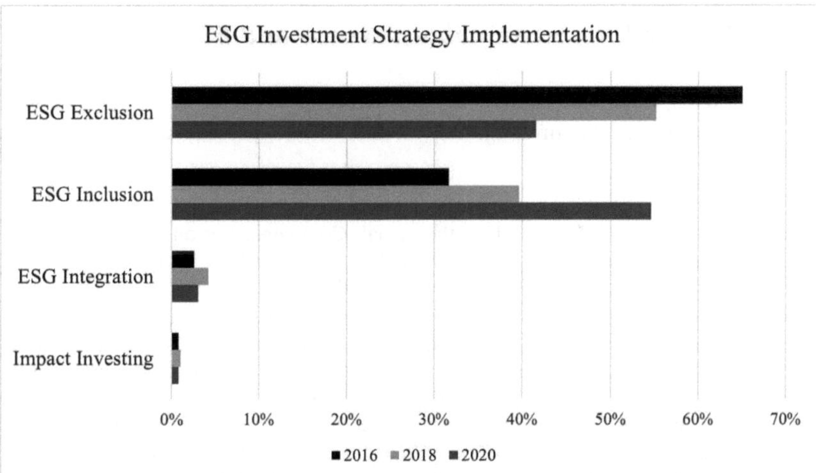

Fig. 2.2 Popularity of Different ESG Investment Strategies. (Note: Own illustration based on data adapted from Global Sustainable Investment Alliance, 2022. The terms ESG Exclusion, Integration, Inclusion, and Impact Investing are further explained in Sect. 2.1.3)

as well as those companies involved in the production of or are linked to the following: controversial weapons, nuclear weapons, and tobacco. The categories of animal testing, abortion and contraception, and stem cell research are only excluded by one index; the oil and gas sector is only excluded by two out of the 10 indices examined. In addition to the already mentioned sectors of controversial weapons, nuclear weapons, and tobacco, conventional weapons, thermal coal, unconventional oil and gas (excluded by nine out of 10 indices series), nuclear power, alcohol, gambling (by six indices), and adult entertainment (by five indices) are excluded by at least half of the analyzed index series.[3] Notably, the indices reserve the right to invest in companies that do not exceed a certain threshold with respect to products or services that are otherwise grounds for exclusion. For example, a turnover threshold could explain why Kesko Oyj and Metro AG, which are both involved in trading and generating turnover from alcohol, are not excluded from the Dow Jones Eurozone Sustainability Screened UCITS Exchange-Traded Funds (ETFs; as of January 5, 2024). The associated index series, the Dow Jones Sustainability Eurozone Index, states that it "excludes companies that derive revenues from alcohol, tobacco, gambling, arms and firearms and/or adult entertainment" (BlackRock, 2024a).

2.1.2 Research in Sustainable Finance and ESG Investing

This section explores the publication trend for research on sustainable finance and ESG investing. The investigation is intended to provide a comprehensive

---

A de-listing is caused by failing to submit the annual "Communication on Progress." According to Knudsen (2011) and Rasche et al. (2018), this is also a matter of company size, which results in a higher likelihood of SMEs getting delisted.

[3] These exclusion criteria exist for the 10 examined SRI and ESG indices and not all SRI and ESG funds have these exclusionary characteristics or invest in all companies belonging to the NSRI sectors. For example, the State Street World ESG Index Equity Fund has invested in NSRI companies as of March 31, 2024. The index fact sheet describes its use of "certain Environmental, Social and Governance (ESG) metrics to tilt the index towards securities demonstrating both a robust ESG profile and a positive trend in improving that ESG profile," as well as excluding "companies that do not meet the portfolio's specified ESG criteria" (State Street Global Advisors, 2024). Another example is an ETF by Blackrock, the iShares ESG Aware MSCI EAFE ETF, which has a stake in Airbus, a company involved in business activities related to nuclear weapons as of March 31, 2024 (BlackRock, 2024b; MBDA, 2023, 2024). With 0.34% of the 401-position portfolio, Airbus falls below their not-strictly-quantified threshold; nuclear weapons fall under "activities classified under 'Minimal Tolerance'" in their methodology (MSCI, 2018). With 1.35%, Shell plc is the 5th largest position in the portfolio (BlackRock, 2024a).

overview of quantitative developments in this domain in recent decades, including an analysis of how sustainable finance research has expanded, diversified, and adapted to global trends and challenges. I illustrate the progression of research on sustainable finance and ESG investing using Paul et al.'s (2021) "scientific procedures and rationales for systematic literature reviews" (SPAR-4-SLR). This review proceeds in three major steps: assembling, arranging, and assessing publications. A more detailed explanation of the characteristics of a holistic SLR is

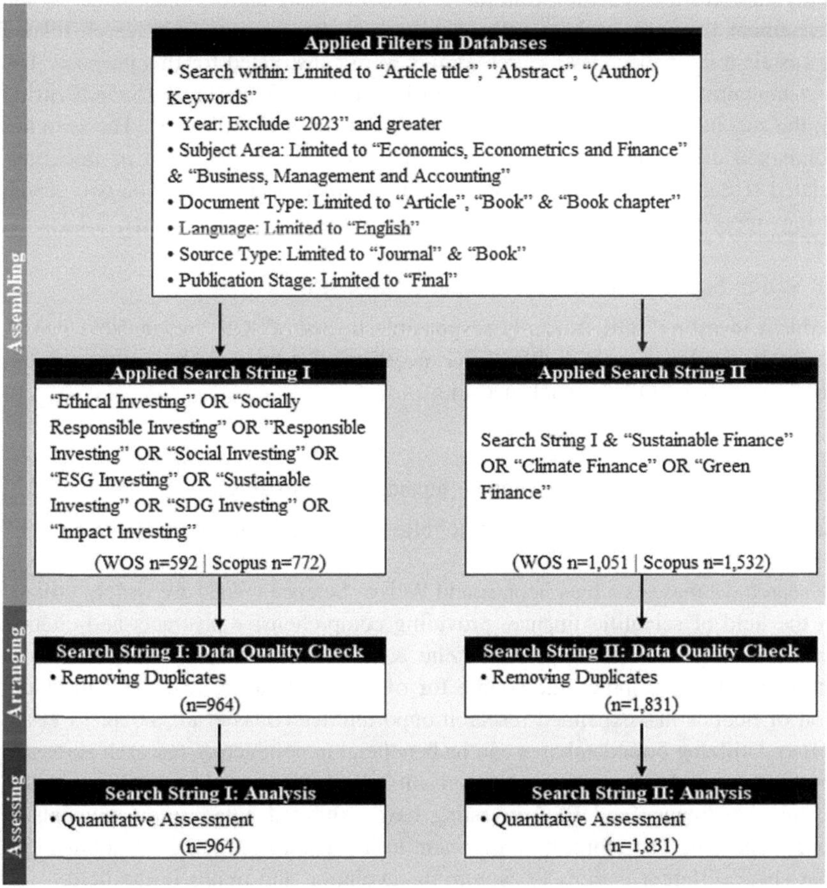

Fig. 2.3 Stages of the Systematic Literature Review (SPAR-4-SLR). (Note: Own illustration)

set out in Sect. 2.2. Given that the primary objective here is to quantify research trends over time rather than engage in a comprehensive review, the structured approach of the SPAR-4-SLR has been employed; see Fig. 2.3 for a depiction of the SPAR-4-SLR process.

2.1.2.1 Assembling Sources

The objective of this phase was to gather relevant publications in the field of sustainable finance and investment, with a specific focus on ESG investing. This study explores the specific evolution of ESG investing and its significance in the investment literature. Additionally, it examines the progress in research related to sustainable finance. Two search strings were constructed for this purpose. The first contains keywords that can be attributed to ESG investing (Search String I); the second includes finance-related keywords (Search String II). The searches conducted using these strings provide an impression of the share of investing-related research within the broader sustainable finance universe. The two search strings reported below are created using the terms mentioned in Sect. 2.1.1.

1) Search String I (the "ESG investing" search string):

"ethical investing" OR "socially responsible investing" OR "responsible investing" OR "social investing" OR "ESG investing" OR "sustainable investing" OR "SDG investing" OR "impact investing"

2) Search String II (the "sustainable finance" search string):

Search String I & "green finance" OR "climate finance" OR "sustainable finance"

Research databases such as Scopus and Web of Science (WoS) are widely utilized in the field of scientific finance, providing comprehensive abstracts and citation data (Harzing & Alakangas, 2016; Zhu & Liu, 2020). While WoS has been a prominent bibliographic data source for over four decades, Elsevier's introduction of Scopus has expanded research opportunities (Baas et al., 2020; Li et al., 2018). Utilizing both databases can be beneficial in conducting research across an extensive period; this study includes results up to 2022. As discussed previously, sustainable finance and ESG investing have exhibited notable developments in recent decades. Therefore, it is important to include a wide range of publications that cover different periods to capture the evolution and trends in the field.

The constraints regarding the field of study are restricted to "economics," "econometrics," "finance," "business," "management," and "accounting." Most studies recommend focusing on articles and excluding books and book chapters as document types due to their content. However, I include books and book chapters in this analysis of the development of sustainable finance as a topic, particularly recognizing the influence of Domini and Kinder's (1984) influential book. Additionally, the language is confined to English, with the source type specified as both "journal" or "book." The publication stage must be marked as "final."

With these criteria and searching within the "article title," "abstract," and "(author) keywords" fields for each database, WoS produced 592 findings for Search String I and 1,051 findings for Search String II. Scopus returned 722 results for Search String I and 1,532 for Search String II. WoS has two keyword search options: "author keywords" and "KeyWords Plus." The former are provided by the authors, and the latter category is a feature of the WoS. The "KeyWords Plus" feature enhances the WoS search capabilities by automatically generating additional keywords based on the content, synonyms, and other terms that are closely associated with the original search query. Since this review is not an in-depth analysis of each paper, I have omitted this feature to avoid unwanted findings. The findings of Zhang et al. (2016) affirm this choice since they argue that KeyWords Plus is as efficient as the author-keywords option but less related to the particular article's content.

2.1.2.2 Arranging the Search Results

In arranging the search results, I have combined the findings of WoS and Scopus for each search string. Following this, duplicate findings were eliminated to ensure the accuracy and integrity of the results. This resulted in 964 findings for Search String I, which reveals the stand-alone nature of ESG investing as a concept. In addition, 1,831 findings were generally related to sustainable finance generated in relation to Search String II. For the purpose of this chapter, the publication trend is more interesting, and no further in-depth analysis has been performed. Section 2.2 presents a comprehensive SLR benefiting the main aim of this research, the relationship between ESG investing and performance.

2.1.2.3 Assessing the Search Results

Figure 2.4 shows that both search strings yielded an increasing number of results over time. There is a significant upward trend in the number of search results for both search strings from around 2010 onwards. Another significant surge can be observed in 2016, following the adoption of the Paris Agreement, along with the endorsement of the 17 global SDGs by the global community under the United Nations Agenda 2030, both of which took place in 2015.

The graph in Fig. 2.4 begins in 1995, as the research output in the preceding years remained consistently between zero and one. It is important to note that the figure does not offer detailed information regarding the content or quality of the research. Its purpose is to present the number of search results obtained for each search string over time, enabling a broad comparison of the trends in research output concerning sustainable finance and ESG investing.

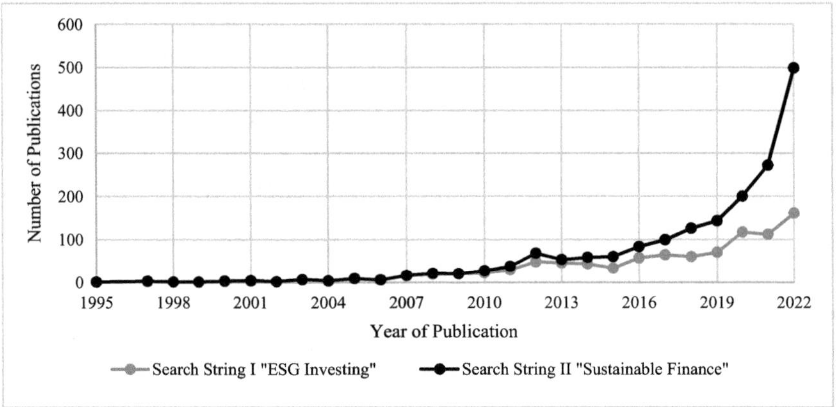

Fig. 2.4 Sustainable Finance Publications for "Finance" and its Subcategory "Investing". (Note: Own illustration)

2.1.3 Types of ESG Investors

There is no consensus regarding how ESG investing and investors should be defined. The only agreement is that these investors take account of ESG-related criteria in their investment decisions. The research question—whether ESG investing comes at the cost of returns—requires that we differentiate between investors who aim for financial returns irrespective of ESG considerations and those who prioritize their investment's ESG impact over financial gains. The transition from ethical investing to SRI and now ESG investing illustrates the progression from simply avoiding certain companies (negative screening) to embracing positive screening and engagement strategies.

This evolution highlights the significant shift toward more proactive approaches in sustainable finance and investment practices. Therefore, it is reasonable to categorize ESG investors who seek competitive financial returns and to reflect their screening and evaluation methods. The financial sector, particularly banking, where meeting the diverse needs of clients is essential, has embraced various approaches to ESG investor classification. For instance, Morningstar Inc. scales investor groups in the range from "avoiding negative outcomes" to "advancing positive outcomes" (Morningstar, 2023). Credit Suisse has developed a Sustainable Investment Framework that involves the exclusion of assets based on the principle of doing no harm and alignment with client values. In addition to exclusion, the framework delineates integration, thematic, and impact approaches (Credit Suisse Group AG, 2023). Similar approaches are identified by institutions that regularly survey ESG investment approaches, prominent institutions such as the UN Principles for Responsible Investment (UN PRI) Association, an UN-supported network of investors, the European Fund and Asset Management Association, the European Sustainable Investment Forum, and the Global Sustainable Investment Alliance.

Table 2.1 categorizes the screening steps by institution (four general financial institutions and two banks) noted above on a scale from "avoid negative outcomes" to "advance positive outcomes." While the institutions refer to this as a screening process, banks present it in the form of action titles. This study builds on existing methods and introduces distinct sub-classifications of ESG investors and precise definitions within each category, thereby contributing to a deeper comprehension of the subject. The "norms-based screening" and "exclusion" approaches both involve excluding companies as potential investment targets. The "best-in-class" approach depends on where the investor has set their focus and might ignore company fundamentals. Thematic investment is more of a preselection of sectors or companies and thus should not be included as a pure ESG screening process.

The ESG screenings of the various institutions analyzed here cover different investment types. This study identifies three possible ESG screening steps: ESG exclusion, ESG inclusion, and ESG integration. The strictness and the extent of an investor's ESG screening steps are independent of their being classified as an ESG investor; what defines an ESG investor is the incorporation of ESG criteria in their investment decisions—along with, in this thesis, the objective of seeking competitive returns. After each of the ESG screening steps, and if not done in advance, an investor may proceed with financial or other analysis.

Table 2.1 Screening Classifications and Investor Approaches. (Note: From Credit Suisse Group AG, 2023; European Fund and Asset Management Association, 2022; Eurosif, 2023; Global Sustainable Investment Alliance; Morningstar, 2023; Principles for Responsible Investment, 2021)

	PRI	EFEMA	EUROSIF	GSIA	Morgan Stanley	Credit Suisse
Avoid negative outcomes	Negative / exclusionary screening	Exclusion	Exclusion	Negative / exclusionary screening	Applying exclusions	Exclusion
	Norms-based screening		Norms-based screening	Norms-based screening	Limiting ESG risk	Integration
	Positive / best-in-class screening	Best-in-class	Best-in-class	Positive / best-in-class screening	Seeking ESG opportunities / best-in-class	
	Sustainability -themed investing	Thematic investment	Sustainability -themed investing	Sustainability -themed investing	Targeting sustainability themes	Thematic
	Integration of ESG issues	ESG integration	ESG integration	ESG integration		
	Active ownership and engagement	Stewardship	Engagement and voting	Corporate engagement and shareholder action	Practicing active ownership	
Advance positive outcomes		Impact	Impact investing	Impact / community investing	Assessing impact	Impact

2.1.3.1 ESG Exclusion

The earliest term associated with shaping today's understanding of the ESG investor is "ethical investing" (see Sect. 2.1.1). ESG exclusion, the first step in ESG investing, involves taking account of ethical considerations regarding the dimensions of ESG. The ESG exclusionary investor aims to achieve competitive returns while consciously avoiding sectors or specific companies that are not in line with the investor's values and ethical principles. The criteria for avoidance may be harmful environmental impact, social irresponsibility, or poor governance of the sector or company.

Section 2.1.1 notes sectors that are categorized as NSRIs, where some asset managers have adopted stricter ethical standards than others. This categorization fits into the present study, which argues that the exclusionary screen is, to some extent, subjective. The Russian invasion of Ukraine has served as a significant test in this regard. While some investors argue that the arms industry destroys lives and is therefore not compatible with ESG principles, others argue for seeing the industry's significance through the lens of the defender. For instance, it is well documented that tobacco causes harm, but it is legal and strictly regulated in most countries of the world. Additionally, the tobacco industry has contributed to economic development, especially in developing economies, through job creation, tax revenue, and agricultural support. The industry has invested in public health initiatives, reduced-risk products, and awareness campaigns about the dangers of smoking. Tobacco companies have also supported community development and education programs. These contributions highlight the industry's complex role in society and efforts to mitigate associated harms.

These two examples show how debatable the nature of the exclusionary screen is in terms of specific sectors. There are different viewpoints through which factors should be considered, leading to the conclusion that the definition of NSRI stocks is subjective, and that one ESG investor may invest in sectors that are excluded by others. In addition to having sector-based considerations, investors can focus on individual metrics for the three ESG dimensions and exclude companies that they perceive to be acting inappropriately, for example, by verifying if they have violated the principles of the UN Global Compact.

2.1.3.2 ESG Inclusion

After excluding unsuitable sectors and/or companies, the ESG inclusionary investor sees the incorporation of ESG considerations as part of the investment analysis. The exclusionary ESG investor excludes companies seen as ESG irresponsible, by contrast ESG inclusion refers to the explicit consideration and inclusion of ESG factors. ESG characteristics are assessed alongside traditional finance metrics and are fully included in the investment process. The investor may set predefined ESG thresholds or criteria and select stocks that meet those. The standards for inclusion may depend on the investor's particular preferences and priorities. The inclusionary approach prioritizes investing in companies that demonstrate proactive ESG engagement, selecting those that not only meet baseline ESG thresholds but also show potential for positive ESG development. This approach reflects an emphasis on investing in companies with solid ESG foundations.

2.1.3.3 ESG Integration

Integration involves evaluating the materiality and relevance of ESG factors to a company's financial performance and long-term sustainability. Investors who integrate ESG into their investment approach analyze business models by company and by sector through an ESG lens to identify opportunities and risks for financial performance. ESG factors are seen as part of the broader investment analysis and are not treated as separate or stand-alone criteria. Integrating ESG factors into the analysis of a company to achieve financial returns involves using ESG criteria to assess the exposure of its financial performance to ESG risks and opportunities. This can be done at a macro level by considering general risks and opportunities, and at a micro level by focusing on a particular company. For example, a company might be avoided due to its exposure to environmental dependencies, such as high water usage in an area where water availability has dropped in recent years.[4] A social risk could be present due to unethical supply chain practices,

[4] These risks and opportunities are also addressed by regulations, such as the Corporate Sustainability Reporting Directive, which requires large companies to report in accordance with the ESRS (see Sect. 1.1). Materiality analysis assesses a company's impacts, risks, and opportunities derived from current or future impacts both on and by ESG factors, as exemplified by "ESRS E1 – Climate Change" (European Financial Reporting Advisory Group, 2023). Additionally, IFRS S2 mandates entities to disclose information about climate-related risks and opportunities that could reasonably be expected to affect the company's cash flows and its access to finance or cost of capital over the short, medium or long term (International Financial Reporting Standards Foundation, 2023). It is important to distinguish between climate-related physical and transition risks. The impact of physical and transition risks also explains why companies may have cheaper access to capital; from the perspective of credit institutions, ESG-related credit risk can be assessed. An example of a physical risk could be climate change leading to a loss of biodiversity and the lack of a viable ecosystem, resulting in reduced agricultural output and affecting the companies' cash-flow. Credit risk increases due to the probability of default and loss given default. A transition risk is the potential consequence of CO_2 emissions contributing to climate change, followed by a higher taxation on CO_2 emissions, impacting the cash flow of CO_2-emission-intensive industries and raising credit risks due to a higher probability of default and loss given default.

which may result in fines and product boycotts. Internally, there is social risk in mistreating employees and losing talent and know-how as a result.[5] With regard to these factors, the investor may also avoid investing in companies potentially facing regulatory pressure in the future. Regulatory tightening tends to burden those companies acting in the same sector that perform less well in ESG terms.

2.1.3.4 Impact Investing

Impact investing is the final screening method included in the model. Impact investors target a measurable impact related to specific ESG criteria or goals, such as a specific SDG. Through their investment, the investor seeks to create meaningful change by directing capital to companies that contribute to specific SDGs or address ESG challenges. The impact investor primarily pursues one overarching goal and has clearly defined key performance indicators (KPIs) that allow them to measure companies' potential contributions toward their SDG or ESG objective. In impact investing, a distinction can be made between the impact investor who invests to generate competitive returns while generating impact, and the investor who prioritizes the impact without aiming for competitive financial returns. Some studies view impact investing as part of ESG investing due to their overlaps. In this dissertation, impact investing is seen as part of sustainable investing, but is distinct from ESG investing, as it specifically aims to advance one or a few SDGs or ESG goals.

2.2 Systematic Literature Review on ESG Investing and Financial Returns

A perfect introduction to this section is from Newman & Gough (2020, p. 3 f.): "Literature reviews can be used for making claims about what we know and do not know about a phenomenon and also about what new research we need to undertake to address questions that are unanswered." In the scholarly literature, numerous studies have explored sustainable investing, ESG investing, and associated classifications, as well as their influence on financial returns. A summary

[5] Numerous studies highlight the significance of a good work environment and employee well-being, particularly emphasizing their impact on younger generations. BlackRock's research indicates that companies boasting low employee turnover tend to outperform companies with high employee turnover across various metrics, including return on assets and revenue per employee (Lawson et al., 2022; MSCI World Index 2012–2021).

of present knowledge and gaps is helpful in examining whether ESG investing entails a trade-off with returns. I consider how other researchers have approached this topic and what conclusions they have reached. This is accomplished through the execution of an SLR, an independent scientific method with roots and a long tradition in medical science; it is first mentioned by Beecher in 1955 in the *Journal of the American Medical Association* (Moher et al., 2009).

The SLR proceeds in phases that have been reformulated from the medical domain to other scientific areas; these phases are sometimes defined differently in different fields (Fink, 2014; Gernsheimer et al., 2021; Khan et al., 2003; Nguyen & Kanbach, 2023). Their common aim is to help researchers systematically evaluate and map the current intellectual landscape to clarify research questions and contribute to existing knowledge (Muka et al., 2020; Tanner-Smith et al., 2019; Tranfield et al., 2003). According to various scholars, an SLR has an organized, transparent, and replicable framework (Chandler & Hopewell, 2013; Higgins, 2020; Penedones et al., 2019; Tanner-Smith et al., 2019; Tranfield et al., 2003).

The methodology has improved over time, especially in the 1990s with the newly created "Cochrane Collaboration," the objective of which was to "prepare, maintain, and disseminate systematic reviews" (Cochrane Library, 2023). Tranfield et al. (2003) revised this methodology and established three stages of conducting an SLR: planning the review (Stage I), conducting the review (Stage II), and reporting and dissemination (Stage III). These stages have often been used in management science. For the purpose of this research, I conducted a diligent and careful, albeit not exhaustive, SLR based on Tranfield et al.'s (2003) three-stage approach. Stage II, conducting the review, was represented by the three major steps of the SPAR-4-SLR model (Sect. 2.1.2), which has been demonstrated to be effective. In Stage III, Steps 4 and 5, derived from the model in Khan et al. (2003), represent the third phase in Tranfield et al.'s (2003) original model, which is a comprehensive research framework focused on "getting evidence into practice." By contrast, this SLR is a constituent part of a research endeavor and seeks to add to existing knowledge (Khan et al., 2003). The approach taken in this research is illustrated in Fig. 2.5.

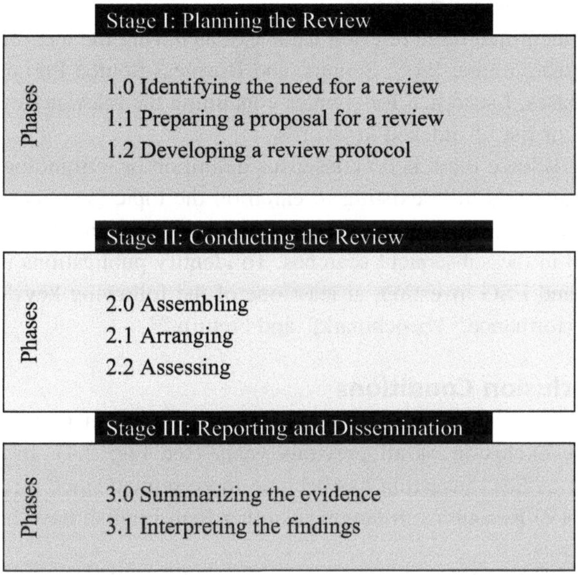

Fig. 2.5 Stages and Phases of a Systematic Literature Review. (Note: Adapted from Khan et al., 2003; Tranfield et al., 2003)

2.2.1 Stage I: Planning the Systematic Literature Review

I address Phase 1.0 (identifying the need for a review) in Sects. 1.1 and 1.2 and Phase 1.1 (preparing a proposal for a review) in Sect. 2.2.

The objective of Phase 1.2 (developing a review protocol) is to safeguard the researcher's objectivity by defining the precise steps to be taken. According to the medical science literature, the researcher derives the review protocol from the defined research objectives (Cochrane Library, 2023). In management research, (Tranfield et al., 2003) propose that a review protocol serves as a safeguard for objectivity by offering detailed outlines of the procedural steps. The review protocol delineates the study's focal questions, the methodology for identifying pertinent studies, and the criteria for including or excluding studies, all while preserving the researcher's capacity for creativity within the review process (Davies & Crombie, 1998). Following this phase, I established the following inclusionary and exclusionary conditions.

2.2.1.1 Inclusion Conditions

Condition I)I identified three relevant databases as having the most holistic coverage of this research area: WoS, Scopus, and Business Source Premier (EBSCO). In these databases, I searched for sources containing the relevant keywords in the title, abstract, or list of indexed keywords.

Condition II)Since there is no consensus definition or terminology in the area of ESG investing and little existing research on the topic (see Sect. 2.1.2.3), the terms and expressions identified during the literature search reported in Sect. 2.1.1 were included in the subsequent searches. To identify publications that deal with performance and ESG investing, at least one of the following keywords must be included: "performance," "benchmark," and "return."[6]

2.2.1.2 Exclusion Conditions

Condition III)Research on ESG investing gained significant traction after 2002, leading to the exclusion of all previous years (see Fig. 2.4). In addition, the understanding of ESG investing has become more refined since then.

Condition IV) Resources in languages other than English have been excluded from the analysis.

Condition V)All published journals were considered. While I did not limit the scope to peer-reviewed journals, I ignored gray literature, including think tank and company publications and book chapters. This follows common research practice, as it ensures a focus on more academically rigorous sources (Adams et al., 2017).

Condition VI)This research focuses on the stock market, and sources were thus excluded where the title or abstract included the following keywords: "debt," "derivative," "bank," "crypto," "loan," and "washing."

Condition VII)Since there has been an upward trend and greater transparency in ESG investing in the last decades (see Sects. 1.1 and 2.1.2) and the European market, in particular, has not been studied often, I did not limit the literature review geographically; however, I excluded studies that focus on one country (except for those focused on the US).

Condition VIII) The SLR does not focus on a specific research method, such as correlation analysis or performance benchmarks, in order to maintain an exploratory approach. Nevertheless, it is important to avoid literature that blends

---

[6] Keywords such as "ESG news," "prediction," and "reaction," which indicate stock market reactions to ESG-related news or changes in reported ESG characteristics, have been not included. These keywords imply an element of speculation, which is inconsistent with the approach of ESG investors and is not the focus of this dissertation. Additionally, the narrow timeframe covered by these reactions may not capture the full extent of their impact.

different definitions of ESG stocks to minimize endogeneity. For a reliable analysis, each study must use a consistent definition of ESG investment methodology to ensure that differences in financial returns are attributable to the specific ESG stock selection process under study. The primary objective is to examine existing analyses and identify any abnormalities in financial returns. Therefore, each study must apply a consistent ESG methodology to maintain the integrity of its findings.

2.2.2 Stage II: Conducting the Review

In Phase 2.0 (assembling), the databases included in accordance with Inclusionary Condition I were searched using keywords and Boolean operators ("AND" and non-strict "OR"). Specifically, investment-related terms were combined using the "OR" operator, and for the second search string, the "AND" operator was employed followed by a combination of the keywords "performance", "benchmark", and "return," which were then joined using an "OR" operator (Inclusionary Condition II). Exclusionary Conditions III–VI were applied to each database. This process yielded over 520 findings.

In the subsequent phase, Phase 2.1 (arranging), the results from the three databases were consolidated, and duplicate studies (210) as well as anonymous publications (1) were removed. Following this process, 309 publications remained for more detailed analysis. This involved reviewing the abstracts and conducting a cursory reading of each publication with a focus on Exclusionary Conditions III–VIII to ensure that any sources that meet these criteria (and were not automatically excluded in the preceding step) are excluded. Exclusionary Conditions VII and VIII were then applied during this phase, resulting in a total of 89 remaining findings. The significant reason that so many studies were excluded is that 56 focused solely on one country (other than the US), and many others did not align with the research topic and analyzed different performance areas or asset classes, such as loans.

In the fourth step of the database searching process, I read the full versions of the remaining 89 publications in detail. Relevant articles were assigned to Group A (7), partially relevant studies to Group B (14), and those that were not relevant to the research objective were assigned to Group C (68) and then excluded. The complete process for Stage II of the SLR is depicted in Fig. 2.6.

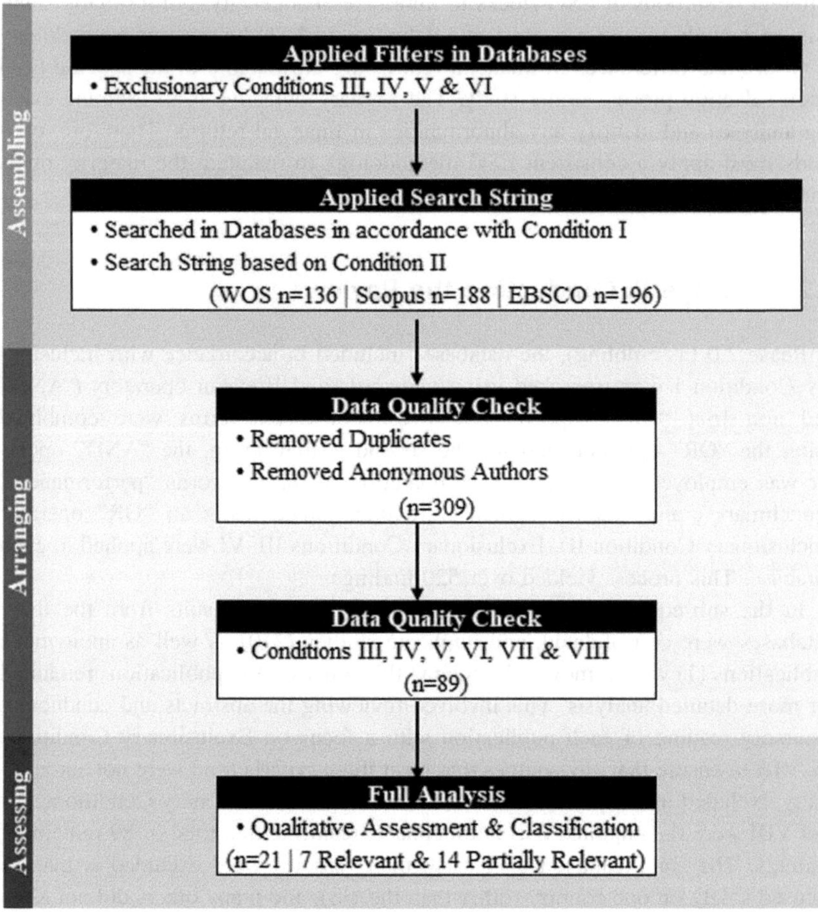

Fig. 2.6 SPAR-4-SLR Processes in Stage II of the SLR. (Note: Own illustration)

2.2.3 Stage III: Result Reporting and Dissemination

In Phase 3.0 (summarizing the evidence), the 21 remaining publications were fully analyzed. Their methodologies and conclusions were summarized in a synoptic overview, with the following information included: title, author(s), year of publication, sample period, covered regions, asset classes, methods, and conclusions. The summaries are set out in Appendix A (ESM), Tables A2 and A3; the journal title, volume, issue, ABS journal ranking, and citations were excluded to keep the tables manageable. An overview of the journals' ABS rankings and main academic disciplines is set out in Fig. 2.7.

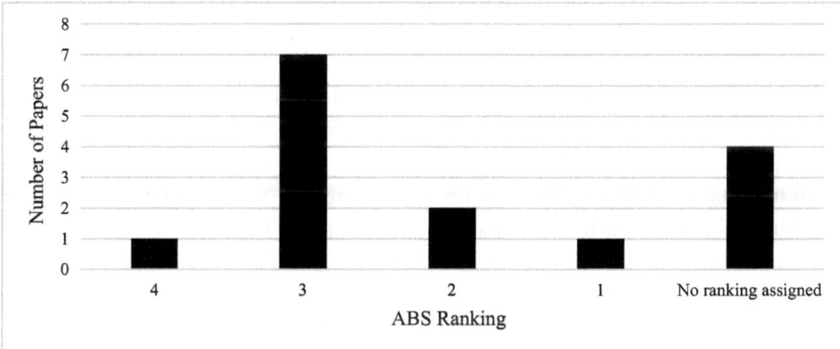

Fig. 2.7 ABS Journal Rankings of the Analyzed Publications. (Note: Not all identified literature was published in journals. Own illustration)

The summary reveals mixed results regarding the link between ESG investing (broadly defined) and its impact on returns.[7] While some studies indicate a positive link between ESG investing and stock market returns, others found no significant relationship or identified a negative relationship.

The research approach varied among the analyzed publications. Twelve considered funds, six focused on stocks, two examined indices, and one analyzed ETFs as primary data sources. Additionally, six publications utilized ESG scores and ratings provided by ESG data providers to compare high- and low-rated companies. The tables reflect the various research methodologies employed, highlighting the range of approaches adopted. These include benchmarking total

[7] Condition VIII specified that only literature utilizing a consistent definition of ESG should be considered. Meta-analyses, which are often subject to endogeneity, were out of scope since they summarized results of studies using different ESG methodologies. An article that is often cited (Atz et al., 2022) is a meta-analysis of studies and found that some ESG strategies generate market-level returns or excess returns when compared to conventional investment strategies and provide downside protection. According to this article, very few studies have found definitive negative correlations between ESG and financial performance. The authors criticize the absence of studies showing why these correlations exist and the missing distinction between different types of investment strategies. Revelli and Viviani (2015) tested the relationship between SRI and financial performance with a meta-analysis of 85 studies; their results indicate that it is neither a weakness nor a strength to follow this approach rather than pursuing traditional investment.

returns of ESG-classified equities against their non-ESG peers, comparisons of financial indicators such as the Sharpe and Treynor ratios, multivariate analysis, and portfolio constructing.

In Phase 3.1 (interpreting the findings), it was found that most studies analyzed ESG or SRI funds and compared their performance with non-ESG benchmarks. However, these studies did not differentiate between the various ESG and SRI classifications or the screening methodologies adopted for these funds, nor did they assess the differences in their investment approaches. As a result of this lack of transparency, it is difficult to interpret the results and draw precise conclusions.

Studies that utilized the ESG scores and/or ratings of companies or funds as a measure of ESG (and thus the basis for investment) relied on the methodologies provided by the ESG data providers. It is thus not possible to draw any conclusions about the impact of specific ESG factors on financial performance, particularly since the methodologies may have changed.

The time horizon of the studies also varies widely, with some focusing on short-term performance and others examining long-term effects. As shown in Sect. 1.1, regulatory pressures have led to greater transparency in regard to ESG information, and the definition of the sub-criteria for ESG has gained traction, especially for European companies; as a result, there is likely more ESG data available. It should be possible to consider the criteria for ESG investing in combination with financial returns. The higher levels of transparency should support a better research focus on ESG criteria than was possible decades or even years ago. An ESG investor could exclude NSRI companies and focus on the ESG sub-criteria that are most relevant for financial performance. If the composition of an ESG portfolio is also determined by ESG scores and ratings, then it is essential to investigate the methodology for calculating these and whether they contain any biases that favor or penalize certain types of firms.

2.3 ESG Rating Providers: Structures and Paradigms

In May 2022, the electric vehicle pioneer Tesla Inc. was removed from the Standard & Poor's (S&P) 500 ESG Index and replaced by the oil refiner Philips 66. A debate has since been brewing about the justification of a company's ESG evaluation by different providers. One of the main criticisms was that while Tesla Inc. was cut from the index, ExxonMobil, one of the world's largest oil and gas companies, was retained and rated in the worldwide top 10 (Kerber & Jin, 2022). This debate suggests that most of the public focus when discussing ESG is on the environmental dimension, with less attention given to the social and governance dimensions.

For transparency, Margaret Dorn, Head of ESG Indices of the S&P Dow Jones Indices, discussed the decision to remove Tesla Inc. in a blog post, highlighting that the global industry group to which Tesla belongs (automobiles and components) witnessed an overall improvement in its average S&P DJI ESG score. Dorn further noted that while Tesla's own S&P DJI ESG score has remained relatively stable in recent years, it was outpaced by the stronger performance of its global industry peers. Some of the factors that influenced Tesla's 2021 S&P DJI ESG score included lower scores for its low carbon strategy ("lack of low carbon strategy") and poor commitment to codes of business conduct. Dorn further pointed to allegations of racial discrimination and poor working conditions at the company. Dorn emphasized Tesla's handling of the National Highway Traffic Safety Administration investigation into multiple deaths and injuries associated with its autopilot vehicles as another factor that had a detrimental impact on the company's S&P DJI ESG score and, consequently, its overall ranking. Dorn concluded that "while Tesla may be playing its part in taking fuel-powered cars off the road, it has fallen behind its peers when examined through a wider ESG lens," which underlines that ESG consists of three dimensions (Dorn, 2023).

One of the key findings in the literature review in Sect. 2.2 is that researchers have utilized portfolio construction as a method for comparing portfolios with higher and lower ESG evaluations. The objective of the following sections is to examine the suitability of ESG scoring and rating providers and their methodologies in the context of portfolio construction.

2.3.1 Popular ESG Rating Providers

The increased demand for ESG investing and reporting, for example, by showing ESG scores, ratings or both, in their reports on investor relations, has presented a market opportunity for numerous new entrants to meet this demand. Environmental Resources Management (ERM), a multinational consultancy firm that focuses on sustainability, reported that, as of 2018, there were over 600 ESG scoring and rating providers, and the number continued to grow (SustainAbility, 2020).[8] Although new players continue to enter the scene, the financial services industry is experiencing consolidation in this business field, with larger firms bringing smaller players under their corporate umbrella. Figure 2.8 highlights some of the notable M&As among ESG scoring and rating providers.

[8] Opimas (2024) expects the ESG data market, which grew by 17% in 2023, to exceed USD 2 billion in 2024. The strong market growth has been especially driven by regulatory impacts (see Sect. 1.1). This growth and demand will continue to attract new market participants

2009	Sustainalytics & Jantzi Research
	Innovest by RiskMetrics Group
	KLD by RiskMetrics Group
	ASSET4 by Thomson Reuters
	New Energy Finance by Bloomberg
2010	The Corporate Library & GMI
	RiskMetrics Group by MSCI
2012	Responsible Research by Sustainalytics
2014	ISS (from MSCI) by Vestar Capital
	GMI Ratings by MSCI
2015	Vigeo & EIRIS
	Russell Indexes by London Stock Exchange
	Ethix SRI Advisory by ISS
2016	Trucost by Standard & Poor
2017	40% of Sustainalytics by Morningstar
	IW Financial by ISS
	South Pole Group investment climate data division by ISS
	ISS (from Vestar Capital) by Genstar Capital
2018	Assets from Solaron Sustainability by Sustainalytics
	oekom research by ISS
2019	Majority stake of Four Twenty Seven by Moody's
	Majority stake of Vigeo Eiris by Moody's
	GES International by Sustainalytics
	FC Business Intelligence by Thomson Reuters
	Beyond Ratings by London Exchange Group
	Carbon Delta by MSCI
	RobecoSAM's ESG ratings by S&P Global
2020	81% stake o ISS by Deutsche Borse
	60% of Sustainalytics by Morningstar
2021	Refinitiv by London Stock Exchange Group
	Center for Social and Sustainable Products by FE fundinfo
2022	The Climate Service by S&P Global
	Shades of Green y S&P Global
	Ethos ESG by ACA Group
2023	The Burgiss Group by MSCI

Fig. 2.8 Merger and Acquisition Activity in the ESG Data Industry. (Note: Mergers are set in boldface; acquisitions in regular type. Own illustration)

In this study, the term "ESG rating provider" refers to providers of ESG scores and those offering ESG ratings. In the financial services industry, there is a distinction between "scoring" and "rating." Credit ratings are expressed as letter grades for businesses and governments, while credit scores are three-digit numbers used in assessing the creditworthiness of individuals and small businesses. In other domains, scoring and rating are used interchangeably. In this dissertation, I adopt "rating" as an umbrella term that encompasses both expressions.

Table 2.2 provides an overview of the providers of the 45 largest ETFs with a regional focus on Europe, alongside the ESG rating providers they use in their methodology. The information about the ESG rating provider used by an ETF

Table 2.2 Largest ETFs in Europe. (Note: Fund sizes retrieved from JustETF.com; rating providers retrieved from ETF fact sheets (as of May 20, 2023))

Rating Provider / ETF Provider	MSCI	Sustain-alytics	ISS	Moody's ESG	Foxberry	Intern	Total (AUM in EUR million)
Amundi	◆	◆					6,298
BlackRock	◆						12,304
BNP Paribas AM	◆			◆		◆	798
Dekabank Group	◆						958
DWS (Xtrackers)	◆		◆				1,660
Invesco	◆						148
Legal & General					◆		92
JPMorgan						◆	579
Ossiam		◆	◆				326
UBS		◆					155
Total (AUM in EUR million)	21,094	1,035	136	66	92	895	

and business models, further driving M&A activities, particularly vertical integration, with established index providers and investment reporting firms acquiring ESG data businesses.

was obtained from the corresponding index websites, where the relevant methodologies are listed and combined at the ETF provider level. BNP Paribas AM and JPMorgan use an internal framework for ESG ratings, leverage ESG data from Foxberry, and perform additional processing.

There is very little information about the market share of ESG rating providers available. According to a 2022 study by Opimas (2022), MSCI, Institutional Shareholder Services (ISS) ESG, and Sustainalytics account for about 60% of the market. According to a non-representative survey conducted by SustAinability in 2020, MSCI and Sustainalytics were the most frequently mentioned providers among 319 sustainability experts (2020b). However, there is a lack of detailed data on the market share of ESG rating providers due to the absence of a common definition and limited financial disclosures by providers regarding the turnover derived from their ESG rating business.

The SLR conducted in Sect. 2.2 has shown that most researchers have used MSCI, Bloomberg, Morningstar, and Refinitiv. The reason for choosing a particular provider or model remains undisclosed in most cases. Prior research suggests the reliability of Google Trends, a service offered by Google, as an additional analytical proxy for investor attention, and it is thus adopted here as an additional analytical approach to estimate the market share of ESG rating providers (Huang et al., 2020). Google Trends can be utilized to determine the market share of ESG rating providers. It provides relative search volumes on a scale from 0 (lowest) to 100 (highest) for individual keywords or in comparisons of multiple keywords within a certain window of time. In case more than one keyword or term is provided, the search value numbers are provided relative to one another.

For this research, the ESG rating providers mentioned in the Opimas report and those frequently referenced in the literature are employed as keywords: Refinitiv ESG, Sustainalytics, MSCI ESG, ISS ESG, S&P ESG, Bloomberg ESG, and ESG Book. Due to Google Trends' five-keyword limitation, each keyword was compared using Sustainalytics as a benchmark over a 12-month period and using the "worldwide" setting for analysis (see Table 2.3). This time frame balances out potential outliers; a too-long sample period may distort the representation of current market share.

Table 2.3 Google Trends Average Interest Numbers Over the Past 12 Months as of 05.16.2023

	Average Interest Number Ratio		
MSCI ESG	77	42	Sustainalytics
Refinitiv ESG	10	60	Sustainalytics
ISS ESG	18	60	Sustainalytics
S&P ESG	38	60	Sustainalytics
Bloomberg ESG	23	60	Sustainalytics
ESG Book	13	60	Sustainalytics

In the next step, I set the average numbers of interest for Refinitiv ESG, ISS ESG, S&P ESG, Bloomberg ESG, and ESG Book in relation to the reference ratio derived from MSCI ESG and Sustainalytics, applying the following formula:

$$Rel_{Keyword} = \frac{42}{Num_{Sustainalytics}} * Num_{Keyword}, \tag{2.1}$$

where $Rel_{Keyword}$ represents the normalized proportion of the investigated keyword for each ESG data provider. The constant 42 is derived from the initial observed ratio between MSCI ESG (77) and Sustainalytics (42). This calculation is performed by dividing the constant (42) by $Num_{Sustainalytics}$, which represents the measured value for Sustainalytics in relation to the investigated keyword. The calculated ratio is then multiplied by $Num_{Keyword}$, representing the measured value for the keyword. This results in the relative distribution of Google Trends data as shown in Table 2.4.

Table 2.4 Google Trends Indication of ESG Rating Providers' Market Share

	$Rel_{Keyword}$	Relative [%]
Sustainalytics	42.00	22.06
MSCI ESG	77.00	40.44
Refinitiv ESG	7.00	3.68
ISS ESG	12.60	6.62
S&P ESG	26.60	13.97
Bloomberg ESG	16.10	8.46
ESG Book	9.10	4.78

Considering Opimas' research (2023), which indicates that MSCI, ISS ESG, and Sustainalytics have a 60% market share, the previous analysis underlines the supremacy of these ESG rating providers (Opimas, 2023). The analysis above shows these providers represent approximately 69% of the market; a reason for this higher percentage could be that only seven out of more than 600 market participants were included in the analysis. This analysis also gives a strong indication that MSCI and Sustainalytics are currently leading the sector.

2.3.2 Analysis of ESG Methodologies and Data

Next, I present prominent ESG rating providers and their models. The in-depth analysis of the ESG rating models offers more information regarding their underlying methodology and data. These firms come from diverse backgrounds, often venturing into ESG ratings from other areas of expertise. Some have roots in the creation of ESG funds; others originated in the realm of data analytics.

2.3.2.1 Refinitiv ESG Scores

Refinitiv, formerly Thomson Reuters Financial & Risk, underwent a spin-off and rebranding process in 2018. It was acquired in 2019 by the London Stock Exchange Group and has since been rebranded (Evening Standard, 2023). Refinitiv provides ESG scores in the form of numerical scores from 0 to 100 and letter grades from D – to A +. The company scores reflect performance on ESG factors relative to other companies in the same sector. There are three types of scores offered by Refinitiv:

- Refinitiv ESG score: This score reflects an assessment of companies based on three pillars (E, S, G) and 10 categories and various data points.
- Refinitiv ESG controversies score: Controversies across all 10 categories are aggregated into one category score.
- Refinitiv ESGC score: This score is a combined score of the ESG score and the ESG controversies scores.

Refinitiv's ESG scores include an industry benchmark, and non-industry indicators are omitted if they are irrelevant for a specific sector. Data are gathered from various other sources, including companies' annual reports, NGO websites, and CSR reports.

In terms of methodology, Refinitiv draws on a vast array of data, including more than 630 distinct ESG metrics. These metrics are clustered into 186 comparable KPIs that are grouped into 10 ESG themes. Refinitiv's final scores are derived from the relative performance of the environmental (E) and social (S) dimensions of a company's specific industry. The governance (G) dimension is evaluated in relation to the country of incorporation.

Refinitiv's ESG controversy score, and thus its ESG combined score (ESGC score) consider 23 distinct controversial ESG topics, including controversies recorded in the most recent completed period. The formula for calculating the ESGC score involves averaging the ESG score and the controversies score where controversies have been recorded. In cases where the controversies score exceeds the overall ESG score, they are considered equal; by design, a company's ESGC score cannot exceed its ESG score (Refinitiv Eikon, 2022).

2.3.2.2 MSCI ESG Rating

MSCI Inc. is a prominent US finance firm renowned for its range of services offered globally. In 2010, MSCI launched its ESG Research division dedicated to evaluating ESG risks and opportunities. It has since grown through acquisitions and is the market-leading provider of ESG ratings according to Opimas and the analysis in Sect. 2.3.1.

The scaling range used by MSCI spans from the best rating of AAA (leader) to the worst rating of CCC (laggard). This enables a comprehensive evaluation of a company's ESG performance within a clear and standardized framework. According to MSCI, its ESG research methodology is designed to assess the most significant ESG risks and opportunities faced by a company and its sector. It measures the company's exposure to these risks and opportunities, assesses the effectiveness of its risk management practices, and compares its overall ESG performance with sector peers globally.

MSCI ESG Research incorporates industry benchmarking that makes it possible to assess companies in the context of their specific industries. The methodology used to calculate the MSCI ESG rating takes into account over 1,000 data points and defines 35 key ESG issues for each industry on a yearly basis. These issues are weighted according to their materiality to ensure a comprehensive assessment.

The data used by MSCI ESG Research are gathered from a variety of sources. Macro data are sourced from academic, government, and NGO datasets, while company disclosures are crucial for collecting specific information. Government databases, media reports, NGO reports, and other stakeholder sources are also used to ensure comprehensive data coverage (MSCI, 2024b).

2.3.2.3 Sustainalytics ESG Risk Rating

Sustainalytics was established in 2008 and acquired by Morningstar in 2020 following the fusion of DSR from the Netherlands, Scores from Germany, and AIS from Spain. Sustainalytics and Morningstar provide two types of ratings:

- Sustainalytics ESG Risk Rating: This is an assessment of a company's ESG risks, both manageable and unmanageable. It is an evaluation of how well the company handles manageable risks and assesses unmanageable risks (Sustainalytics, 2020).
- Morningstar ESG Risk Rating: This is a visualization of the Sustainalytics ESG Risk Rating using a five-globe logic. A higher number of globes indicates lower ESG risk. The number of globes a company or a fund is awarded is determined relative to other funds within the same Morningstar Global Category. This implies that even if one company or fund faces higher ESG risks than another, it may still receive a better rating if it belongs to a global category with relatively high levels of ESG risk (Morningstar, 2021).

In this dissertation, I concentrate on the Sustainalytics ESG Risk Rating due to its greater precision. The Sustainalytics ESG Risk Rating spans from 0 (negligible) to 40 + (severe), which enables a thorough assessment of a company's ESG risk profile within a standardized framework.

The Sustainalytics methodology considers 138 unique sub-industry classifications. The impact of 20 material ESG issues is considered for each sub-industry, and the impact of the main 10 material ESG issues is considered across all sub-industries. If a particular material ESG issue is not relevant to a company, it may be excluded from the analysis.

The data for the ESG Risk Rating are collected from various sources. Sustainalytics collects information from public documents available on the issuer's website and from regulatory authorities and trusted NGOs. Direct communication with issuers contributes significantly to ensuring accurate and up-to-date data.

Sustainalytics and Morningstar's ESG ratings offer industry benchmarking, enabling the assessment of companies within an industry-specific framework. This allows for comparison against industry peers (Morningstar, 2021; Sustainalytics, 2020).

2.3.2.4 ISS ESG Corporate Rating

ISS ESG is a subsidiary of ISS, which is the leading proxy advisor to investment management firms regarding voting matters during the annual proxy vote.

Deutsche Boerse acquired an 81% controlling interest in ISS ESG in 2021 after it was sold by MSCI to a private equity firm.

Among the six ESG ratings provided by ISS ESG, the ESG Corporate Rating is particularly relevant in this research. This rating concentrates on assessing companies at the individual level, making it a fitting option for analysis. This rating takes a sector-specific approach that emphasizes the materiality of non-financial data. The assessment takes into account ESG risks and opportunities across the entire company value chain.

The ISS ESG rating scale spans from the highest rating of best (A +) to the lowest rating of worst (D −). Similar to other scoring and rating systems, it benchmarks ESG performance relative to industry peers, which makes direct comparisons across industries difficult. The methodology itself relies on over 800 indicators, including a set of 100 indicators specific to each sector. In each sector, four or five material issues are emphasized and given greater weight in the assessment process. The decile rank is used to indicate a company's performance relative to its industry peers.

The data for ISS ESG ratings are derived from various sources. Controversy assessment involves evaluating data from 4,500 selected media outlets and more than 150 stakeholder sources. Data are collected from annual reports, including CSR reports, public websites, and direct communications with rated companies every two to three years (ISS, 2023).

2.3.2.5 S&P Global ESG Score

S&P Global Inc. was originally established in the media sector and transitioned into the financial services sector through the acquisition of S&P. The company is widely renowned for its corporate credit ratings. S&P Global's ESG Scores offer a comprehensive assessment, grading companies on a scale from 0 to 100, with higher scores indicating better performance. The ESG Scores provided by S&P Global go beyond evaluating companies' engagement and performance with respect to key ESG risks and opportunities; they also take into account the quality and completeness of their public disclosures. S&P Global's ESG Scores incorporate up to 30 focus areas across each ESG dimension and address 130 sustainability topics using up to 1,000 data points tailored to individual industries. The aim is to provide an in-depth assessment of a company's overall sustainability performance relative to its industry peers.

The data for S&P Global ESG Scores are predominantly public company data and data drawn from direct interactions with the companies (S&P, 2022; S&P, 2024).

2.3.2.6 Bloomberg's ESG Scores

The methodology for calculating Bloomberg's ESG score was not extensively detailed at the time of this research. Bloomberg has collected and aggregated a range of company ESG data and has also launched a proprietary ESG score. It was thus an ESG data service provider before it became an ESG score provider. Bloomberg's numerical scale ranges from 0 to 10, with higher scores indicating better ESG performance. Each ESG dimension is evaluated separately, and industry-specific materiality factors are considered when assessing companies. Like that of other providers, Bloomberg's methodology involves the processing of reported data, derived ratios, and sector- and country-specific information. It references up to 12 years of historical data spanning over 900 fields covering various sustainability topics such as air quality, climate change, water, and energy management. This is done by identifying the most relevant environmental and social criteria for each sector.

The data utilized for these scores are derived from publicly available company data such as CSR and annual reports, proxy statements, corporate governance reports (governance data only), company websites, CDP data, and direct communications with company representatives. According to Bloomberg, only comparable data are included. Companies may be penalized for missing or incomplete data (Bloomberg LP, n.d.).

2.3.2.7 ESG Performance Score by ESG Book

Arabesque Partners, a German and British investment management firm, introduced Arabesque S-Ray 2018, which was renamed the ESG Book in 2022 (ESG Book, 2022). The primary objective of the ESG score offered by ESG Book is to assess a company's stance on financially material sustainability issues. The methodology for determining the ESG score concentrates on evaluating the influence on financial materiality. This means that when appraising a company's ESG score, the ESG Book algorithm gives priority to data that have a substantial impact on predicting future risk-adjusted performance. Greater weight is given to characteristics considered more material, with these weights rebalanced on a rolling quarterly basis. The resulting ESG score ranges from 0 to 100, with 50 representing the neutral midpoint. Scores exceeding 50 signify robust performance, and scores below 50 indicate that a company has room for improvement.

ESG Book's scores are updated daily, with new data incorporated as soon as they become available. The algorithm integrates over 250 metrics to provide a sector-specific assessment of public companies' performance on financially material sustainability factors. Companies with insufficient data are not given scores, and data quality is checked daily to identify and remove poor-quality data. Sparse or infrequent time series are estimated and adjusted for daily calculations. These measures ensure that ESG Book's scores are accurate and reliable, allowing investors to make informed decisions based on company sustainability (ESG Book, 2023).

2.3.2.8 Initial Insights for a Quantitative Analysis

A comprehensive synoptic overview of the primary discoveries is reported in Appendix A (ESM), Table A4. After a thorough qualitative analysis, I carry out a quantitative investigation before drawing conclusions and highlighting the implications of this research. Section 2.1.1 demonstrated that the lack of an agreed-upon definition of ESG investing leads to various subjective interpretations. In Sect. 2.1.3, various types of ESG investors were discussed. Before delving into deeper conclusions, I offer some initial insights that are important for the following quantitative analysis. ESG rating providers assign different weights to different data points but also consider different perspectives. As their names suggest, some assessments are labeled as "scores," and others are labeled as "ratings." The analysis indicates that some providers score specific areas of ESG performance, while others rate the influence of ESG risks on the company's business model and creditworthiness. There are also approaches that combine these methods.

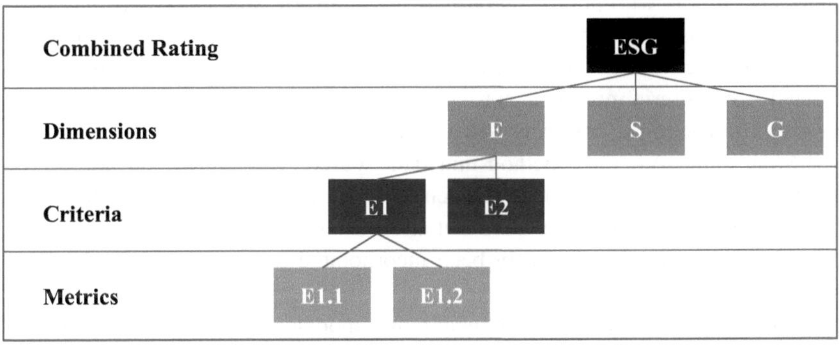

Fig. 2.9 Typical Anatomy of an ESG Rating Model. (Note: Own illustration)

What these rating models have in common is their typical anatomy, depicted in Fig. 2.9. The combined rating is produced by aggregating individual ratings for each ESG dimension, which are also published by some ESG rating providers. Relevant criteria are identified to assess each ESG dimension. Each criterion is then assessed using multiple metrics. The specific metrics are either binary indicators or numerical values. For instance, in the environmental dimension, a criterion could be "climate change impact." This criterion can be assessed using metrics like "greenhouse gas emissions," "percent of renewable energy consumption," or "efforts to mitigate climate change." While the first two of these are quantifiable, the metric, "efforts to mitigate climate change," is an example of a binary "yes/no" determination. Another example of an environmental criterion is "biodiversity conservation," where "impact on biodiversity" and "efforts to protect biodiversity" are two applicable metrics.

Individual weightings typically exist between each stage. ESG metrics are differently weighted for the calculation of the criteria, the criteria are differently weighted for determining each dimension rating, and all dimensions are differently weighted to obtain the ESG combined rating.

2.3.3 ESG Ratings and STOXX Europe 600

Among the various types of ESG investors (Sect. 2.1.3), those who exclude companies and sectors with poor ESG ratings or that are classified as NSRI may have their own exclusion criteria. Other investors may require more detailed information about specific ESG attributes than an ESG rating provides. While some selected ESG criteria may be quantifiable, others—such as the evaluation of controversies impacting a company—require a qualitative evaluation. In Appendix A (ESM), Table A4, the "method and data source" row shows the number of data points or attributes considered when determining the underlying rating. This implies that the ESG characteristics that an investor selects based on their subjective assessment may have already been incorporated and processed by the ESG rating agency.

ESG rating providers consider their rating models as valuable tools for providing aggregated information through a combined rating of the three ESG dimensions or even individual ratings for each dimension. In Sect. 2.3.1, various providers were mentioned, and Sect. 2.3.2 delved deeper into their methodology. Moreover, the evolution of SRI and ESG investing (Sect. 2.1.1) shows the absence of a clear-cut definition of attributes that classify a company as positive or negative in ESG terms; this subjectivity is also apparent in rating methodologies. As a result, differences in the outcomes of the ESG rating providers are anticipated.

2.3.3.1 Data and Methods

Among others, the articles "Aggregate confusion: The divergence of ESG ratings" (Berg et al., 2019) and "Divergent ESG ratings" (Dimson et al., 2020) have analyzed the ratings offered by various ESG rating providers, specifically for US stocks, and found significant differences between their evaluations. Given the extensive regulatory frameworks and applicable reporting standards, it is important to investigate ESG ratings in the context of European public companies. The following analyses address this gap in the literature.

The STOXX Europe 600 Index is widely diversified, with 600 shares from 18 European countries as of February 2023. It thus provides a suitable basis for analyzing ESG rating providers. This study uses as its sample the stocks comprising the STOXX Europe 600 as of February 10, 2023. The ESG ratings of the 600 companies from the providers discussed in Sect. 2.3.1—Bloomberg, ESG Book, ISS, MSCI, Refinitiv (ESG score and ESG combined score), S&P, and Sustainalytics—were collected directly from the provider websites or terminals on February 10, 2023. The data analysis and visualization were conducted using a combination of tools, primarily the R programming language in RStudio. The ggplot2 and ggstatsplot R libraries were crucial for enhanced analysis and visualization and extensive exploration of the dataset. Microsoft Excel was used for simple calculations and data organization.

The ratings provided by MSCI and ISS are reported in letter grades; therefore, they were converted into numerical ratings for analysis purposes. The MSCI ESG ratings range from the highest rating, AAA, to the lowest, CCC. In this specific dataset of STOXX Europe 600-listed stocks, the highest rating assigned by MSCI ESG was AAA, with B being the lowest allocated rating. Similarly, ISS uses a grading system with ratings ranging from A + (highest) to D − (lowest). Using this system, a rating of A − was the best rating assigned, and the worst rating assigned was a D. The use of letter rankings suggests an ordinal rather than an interval scale since the distances between the letters do not correspond to precise numerical values. However, by employing numerical values (see Tables 2.5 and 2.6), these ratings can be used for quantitative analysis since they maintain a linear relationship.

Table 2.5 MSCI ESG Letter Ratings Converted to Numerical Values

MSCI ESG Letter Rating	Assigned Numerical Value
AAA	1.000
AA	0.800
A	0.600
BBB	0.400
BB	0.200
B	0.000

Table 2.6 ISS ESG Letter Ratings Converted to Numerical Values

ISS ESG Letter Rating	Assigned Numerical Value
A −	1.000
B +	0.875
B	0.750
B −	0.625
C +	0.500
C	0.375
C −	0.250
D +	0.125
D	0.000

A variable reversal was necessary to achieve data integrity and standardization. Sustainalytics' ratings underwent min–max normalization to perform the variable transformation, which was achieved with the following formula:

$$x' = \frac{x - max(x)}{min(x) - max(x)}, \tag{2.2}$$

where x represents the rating assigned to a specific stock by Sustainalytics, *max(x)* denotes the highest (worst) rating, and *min(x)* represents the lowest (best) rating. For this dataset, *max(x)* was 47.49 and *min(x)* was 4.70. A proportionate value was obtained by deducting the minimum value from the original value and dividing it by the range. Upon application of this formula, the maximum rating was transformed to 0, and the minimum rating was transformed to 1. Through this reversal, the best rating assigned by Sustainalytics is now represented by 1, and the worst rating is represented by 0.

As outlined in Sect. 2.3.2 on the methodologies of ESG rating providers, there are two main approaches to assessing companies in an ESG context: a risk-rating approach and the ESG-performance rating approach.[9] Considering these approaches is essential, as they represent two distinct approaches—or three, if combined. Previous studies have neglected this aspect.

A second crucial takeaway from the qualitative analysis is that most providers' calculations incorporate a sector benchmark. Thus, there is a high probability that the ratings of two providers are different simply because they have analyzed a different number of companies within a sector, resulting in a different benchmarking scope. However, despite differences in the analyzed scope, the ranking should remain consistent, suggesting a nonlinear relationship between the ratings of different providers. As a result, the available data exhibit characteristics of an interval scale. This means that while specific numerical values may not be directly comparable across providers, their rankings can still serve as the basis for comparative analysis and decision-making. This can be analyzed by calculating the intraclass correlation coefficient (ICC). In addition, the Pearson correlation coefficients should also be calculated.

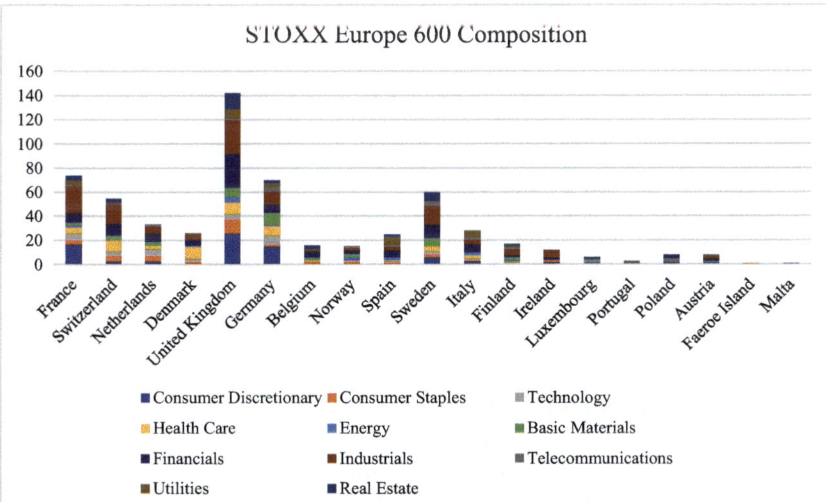

Fig. 2.10 Composition of the STOXX Europe 600 as of 10.02.2023. (Note: Own illustration)

[9] As previously noted, in this dissertation, the terms "rating" and "scoring" are used interchangeably, as they are in other domains, with "rating" serving as an umbrella term encompassing both concepts.

Table 2.7 ICB Sector and Supersector Distribution in the STOXX Europe 600

ICB Sector	ICB Supersector	Stocks	Share
Basic materials	Basic resources	18	7.00%
	Chemicals	24	
Consumer discretionary	Automobiles and parts	14	13.50%
	Consumer products and services	32	
	Media	11	
	Retail	11	
	Travel and leisure	13	
Consumer staples	Food, beverage, and tobacco	30	7.67%
	Personal care, drug, and grocery stores	16	
Energy	Energy	21	3.50%
Financial	Banks	42	17.67%
	Financial services	33	
	Insurance	31	
Healthcare	Healthcare	56	9.33%
Industrial	Construction and materials	24	21.17%
	Industrial goods and services	103	
Real estate	Real estate	36	6.00%
Technology	Technology	33	5.50%
Telecommunications	Telecommunications	22	3.67%
Utilities	Utilities	30	5.00%

The STOXX Europe 600 consists of 600 companies from 18 countries, covering a total of 11 sectors and 20 supersectors in the Industry Classification Benchmark (ICB) taxonomy. Figure 2.10 displays the stock distribution across countries and ICB sectors, while Table 2.7 provides details on the stocks belonging to each ICB sector and ICB supersector. This diversity and representation of various sectors and countries in the STOXX Europe 600 index allows for a comprehensive analysis of ESG ratings across sectors.

2.3.3.2 General Correlation

In the initial phase of the quantitative analysis, I conducted a comprehensive examination of the correlations among the various combined ESG ratings for the stocks comprising the STOXX Europe 600. This analysis aims to demonstrate the intricate relationships between the rating provided by the various providers. As the data exhibit characteristics ordered on an interval scale and the aim is to evaluate the linear relationship between variables, the Pearson correlation coefficient (r) was calculated to measure the correlations. The Pearson correlation coefficient is a robust measure of the strength and direction of the linear relationship between two variables. The correlation coefficient ranges from −1 to 1, where a value of −1 indicates a perfect negative correlation, 0 indicates no correlation, and a value of 1 indicates a perfect positive correlation. The following formula was applied for each combined ESG rating:

$$r = \frac{\sum(x_i - \overline{x})(y_i - \overline{y})}{\sqrt{\sum(x_i - \overline{x})^2 \sum(y_i - \overline{y})^2}}, \tag{2.3}$$

where x_i and y_i denote the individual combined ESG ratings of the STOXX Europe 600 companies from two providers, and the $\overline{x}$ and $\overline{y}$ represent the mean values of the respective underlying datasets. Stocks without a rating from either provider were excluded from the analysis. The resulting r quantifies the linear

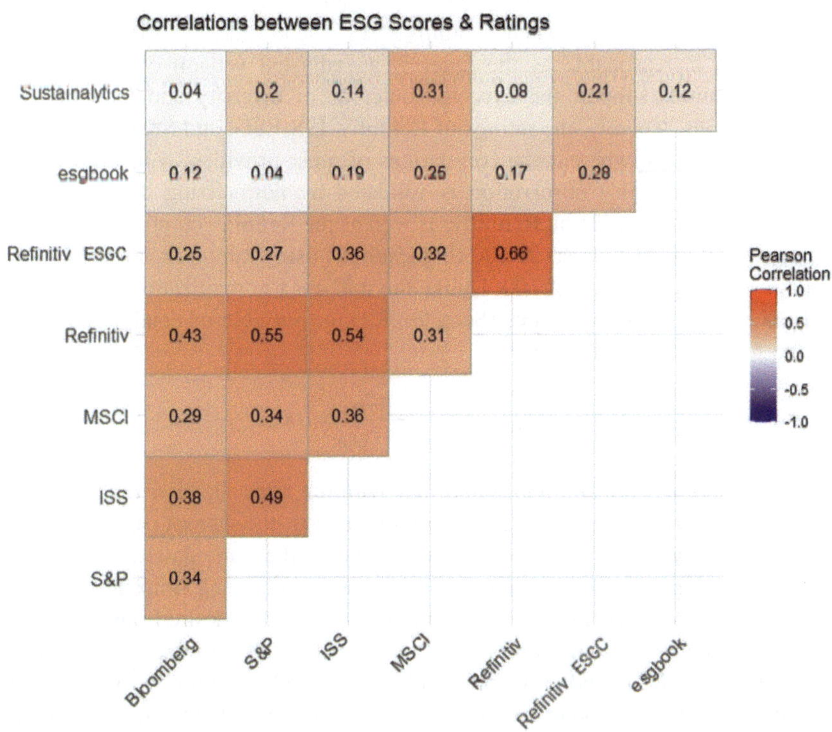

Fig. 2.11 Correlation Coefficients Between ESG Rating Agencies for STOXX Europe 600 Stocks. (Note: Own illustration)

relationship between the combined ESG ratings provided by the two analyzed ESG rating providers.

As depicted in Fig. 2.11, all correlation coefficients were positive. However, the low correlation coefficient of 0.04 between Sustainalytics and Bloomberg and between ESG Book and S&P suggests almost no association between them. The qualitative comparison of Sustainalytics and Bloomberg shows differences in their methodologies: one assesses ESG risks, while the other provides an ESG score. S&P employs a mixed methodology for evaluating companies' engagement and performance on key ESG risks and opportunities, whereas ESG Book assesses how well companies are positioned for financial outperformance by considering factors relevant to future profitability. Despite the various options for data analysis and weighting available to providers, these different perspectives, to some degree, explain the minimal association between their measures.

Besides the above, primarily moderate correlations are evident. The strongest correlation identified is between Refinitiv's ESG score and its ESG combined score, which is reasonable as the latter is an adjusted version of the former. Other correlations support the expected outcome of diversity and moderate to low correlations. Notably, the ratings of Refinitiv, ISS ESG, and S&P exhibit the highest correlations, whereas the correlations of other providers with ESG Book are slightly lower. This observation is validated by normalizing the combined ESG ratings of S&P, ISS, and Refinitiv, as well as the Refinitiv combined score on a scale from 0 (lowest/worst) to 100 (highest/best) using min–max normalization by adding a multiplication of 100. Unlike the min–max normalization applied for the ESG ratings of Sustainalytics (Sect. 2.3.3.1), no variable reversal is required, and the formula is thus as follows:

$$x_{normalized} = \frac{x - x_{min}}{x_{max} - x_{min}} * 100, \tag{2.4}$$

where x represents the original value that requires normalization on the scale from 0 to 100, $x(min)$ denotes the minimum value in the dataset of each rating provider, and $x(max)$ denotes the maximum value in the same dataset.

First, the range of ratings is standardized to a scale ranging from 0 to 1. This result is then multiplied by 100 to rescale the value to the desired range of 0 to 100. This min–max normalization procedure is used for all combined ESG ratings provided by ISS, S&P, and both combinations provided by Refinitiv to transform all rating data into a standardized range between 0 and 100. This normalization facilitates the visual comparison of ESG ratings. A scatter plot was generated using RStudio to represent the standardized ESG ratings. This plot provides a graphical depiction of the relationships and patterns of the three providers with the highest correlation coefficients. As there is a strong correlation between the Refinitiv datasets, the ESG score was selected at random as the independent variable and represented on the x-axis (see Fig. 2.12).

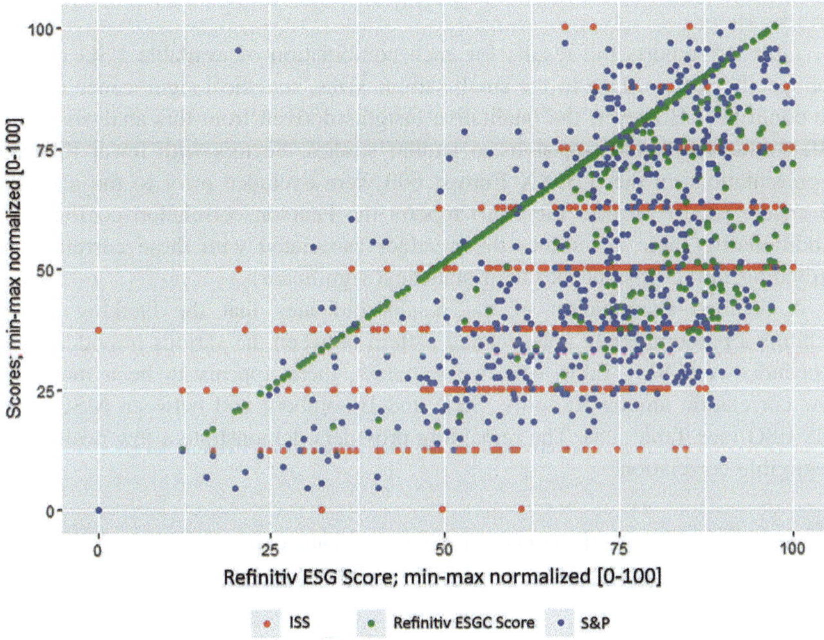

Fig. 2.12 Scatterplot of Normalized ESG Rating from Highly Correlated Providers. (Note: Own illustration)

From the correlation between the two Refinitiv ESG scores, we can infer a significant downgrade of certain companies based on their level of controversy. The visualization in Fig. 2.12 illustrates how the controversy variable has resulted in several downgrades. Due to the initial narrow range of the ISS ESG rating, ranging from 1 to 9 before normalization, it was anticipated that the scatterplot would show a gradual pattern.

2.3.3.3 Correlations Within Sectors

After calculating the Pearson correlations for the entire STOXX Europe 600 dataset, I proceeded with an analysis on a sector basis utilizing the well-established ICB taxonomy. The intention is to investigate the relationships of the combined ESG ratings within individual sectors. Two primary considerations provide the rationale for this approach. First, by using different weightings and selection criteria, the rating agencies' methodologies are sector-specific. Second, the analysis unveils the differences in correlation values between Refinitiv's ESG score and its ESGC score, which includes the ESG controversy score, across diverse sectors.

Table A5 reports the results for each combination of available ESG ratings for specific sectors. Due to the small sample sizes, statistical significance cannot be confirmed. However, the qualitative insights derived from this analysis could offer value for meta-regressions in similar studies. Sectors with fewer than 20 representations in the STOXX Europe 600 were excluded prior to the analysis to ensure robust results. Table A6 reports the Pearson correlation coefficients. Additionally, Table A7 shows the p-values associated with these correlations, providing further insight into their statistical significance.

A detailed examination of the results indicates that the banking sector exhibits a predominantly uncorrelated pattern between the various providers (see Appendix A (ESM) Table A6). Nevertheless, there appears to be a modestly low correlation among Refinitiv, S&P, and Bloomberg and between MSCI and ISS ESG (see Table 2.8). The remaining providers demonstrate a low positive to negligible correlation.

Table 2.8 Pairs with the Highest Correlation in the Banking Sector

Banking (ICB Sector)					
Providers	r	n	t	df	p
Refinitiv (ESG Score)–S&P	0.50	21	2.52	19	0.021
Refinitiv (ESG Score)–Bloomberg	0.50	22	2.55	20	0.019
S&P–Bloomberg	0.56	19	2.76	17	0.013
MSCI–ISS ESG	0.59	19	3.04	17	0.007

One possible explanation is that it is very difficult to select specific and precise criteria for evaluating banks' ESG practices. It is challenging to obtain comprehensive information for a service company that invests funds and provides loans or credits for projects that are mostly not publicly visible. Negative information regarding bank practices often comes to light through third parties and is then shared in the media. While not all banks engaged in such practices, many have been at the center of major financial crises not only because of their irresponsible lending and risky financial practices but also because of questionable ethics and governance practices. A strong indicator of the high number of controversies is the low correlation coefficient of 0.22 between Refinitiv's ESG scores and ESGC scores. This suggests a substantial downgrade of companies within the banking sector by the controversy layer of Refinitiv (see Table 2.9). The associated p-value is 0.164, which is greater than the significance level of 0.05. Hence, the correlation is not statistically significant at the 5% level. The lack of statistical significance suggests that any observed connection between these ratings is random.

Table 2.9 Correlation Coefficients Between Refinitiv's ESG Scores and ESG Combined (ESGC) Scores by Sector

Refinitiv ESG Scores–Refinitiv ESG Combined Scores					
Sector (ICB)	r	n	t	df	p
Pharmaceuticals and biotechnology	0.50	29	3.03	27	0.005
Software and computer services	0.93	23	11.25	21	0.000
Chemicals	0.93	24	11.60	22	0.000
Banks	0.22	42	1.42	40	0.164
Non-life insurance	0.42	21	1.99	19	0.061
Medical equipment and services	0.68	24	4.36	22	0.000
Investment banking and brokerage services	0.81	30	7.30	28	0.000
Construction and materials	0.49	24	2.62	22	0.016
Industrial engineering	0.79	20	5.48	18	0.000
Industrial support services	0.83	26	7.29	24	0.000
Real estate investment trusts	1.00	21			0.000

Table 2.10 Pearson Correlation Coefficients for the Environmental Dimension Among ESG Rating Providers

	Refinitiv ESG Score	S&P	Bloomberg	esgbook
Refinitiv ESG Score	1.00	0.48	0.27	0.63
S&P	0.48	1.00	0.31	0.42
Bloomberg	0.27	0.31	1.00	0.16
esgbook	0.63	0.42	0.16	1.00

Table 2.11 Pearson Correlation Coefficients for the Social Dimension Among ESG Rating Providers

	Refinitiv ESG Score	S&P	Bloomberg	esgbook
Refinitiv ESG Score	1.00	0.52	0.25	0.50
S&P	0.52	1.00	0.25	0.31
Bloomberg	0.25	0.25	1.00	0.12
esgbook	0.50	0.31	0.12	1.00

Table 2.12 Pearson Correlation Coefficients for the Governance Dimension Among ESG Rating Providers

	Refinitiv ESG Score	S&P	Bloomberg	esgbook
Refinitiv ESG Score	1.00	0.30	0.40	−0.09
S&P	0.30	1.00	0.22	−0.19
Bloomberg	0.40	0.22	1.00	0.04
esgbook	−0.09	−0.19	0.04	1.00

The sector-specific correlation between Refinitiv's ESG scores and ESG combined scores also shows that there is a perfect positive correlation within the "real estate investment trusts" sector. This suggests that there are no controversies concerning the 21 companies in this group and indicates a strong alignment with responsible and sustainable business practices.

2.3.3.4 Correlations Within Dimensions

The examination of correlations between combined ESG ratings revealed notable cross-sectoral differences. The Pearson correlations are calculated for each of the ESG dimension ratings, namely environmental rating, social rating, and governance rating. Not all ESG rating providers offer these dimensional ratings; this analysis includes the dimensional ratings of Refinitiv, S&P, Bloomberg, and ESG Book. All models from these providers are classified as ESG-performance rating models and do not solely assess risk; particularly noteworthy is that ESG Book places greater emphasis on a company's potential for future financial outperformance. The Pearson correlation coefficients reflecting the relationships among the various ESG rating models are found in Tables 2.10 to 2.12. All ratings are normalized.

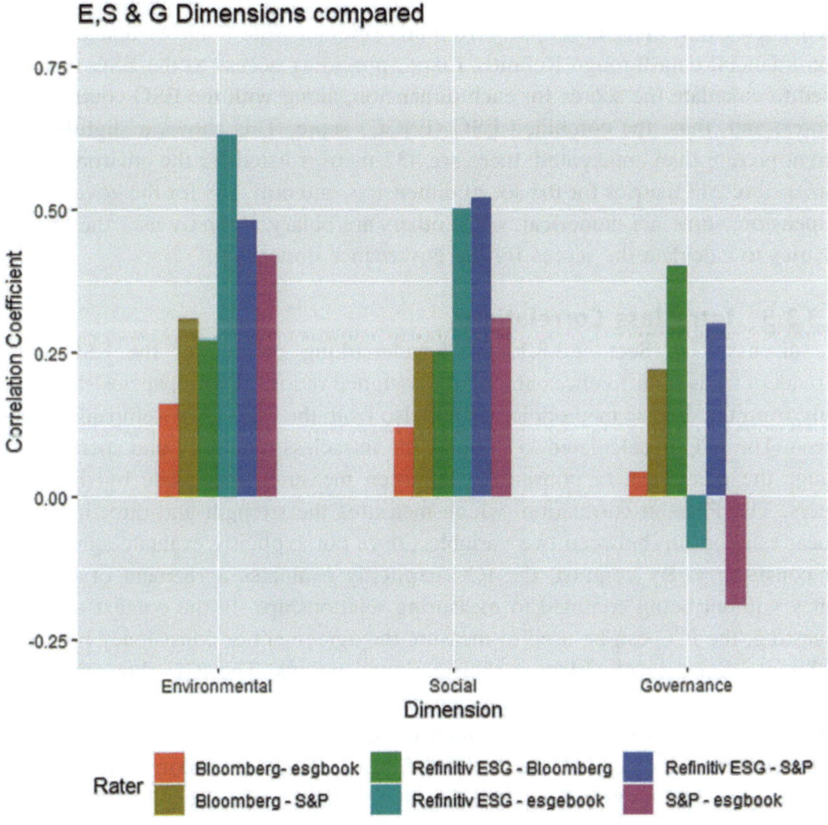

Fig. 2.13 Correlation of ESG Rating Providers by ESG Dimension. (Note: Own illustration)

As shown in Fig. 2.13, the Pearson correlation coefficients show the highest level of consensus for the environmental dimension and the lowest for the governance dimension. This low consensus for the governance dimension is somewhat surprising, as compared to the other dimensions, governance has a richer and longer history of investor interest and reporting. Therefore, one might have expected higher data quality and availability, leading to a high level of consensus. This may be due to ESG data providers having access to the same data for the other two dimensions, due to their limited availability. In particular, the correlation between ESG Book and other providers is negative to nonexistent, which might be explained by the fact that ESG Book's methodological statement focuses on financial impacts. Refinitiv offers a wide range of financial and non-financial data through Refinitiv Eikon, providing access to the ESG metrics used to calculate the scores for each dimension, along with the ESG controversy scores, and, thus, the combined ESG (ESGC) score. This shows a slightly different picture than anticipated: there are 437 metrics listed for the environmental dimension, 248 metrics for the social dimension, and only 158 for the governance dimension; some are numerical, while others are binary. Refinitiv uses the fewest metrics to calculate the scores for the governance dimension.

2.3.3.5 Intraclass Correlations

As discussed in Sect. 2.3.3.1, the benchmarking process of the ESG data providers leads to differences among the assigned ratings. Discrepancies stem not only from the diverse methodologies but also from the number of companies analyzed. The ICC is calculated to evaluate the intraclass reliability and specifically gauge the agreement or consistency between measurements made by different raters. The Pearson correlation, which measures the strength and direction of a linear relationship between two variables, does not explicitly evaluate agreement or consistency. By contrast, the ICC explicitly evaluates agreement or consistency without being confined to measuring relationships. In the context of ESG investing, the ICC can be used to measure the agreement or consistency between different ESG data providers in their assigned ratings. The ICC shows if more than two (i.e., at least three) rating providers deliver the same or at least similar judgments and the extent to which these judgments align. This calculation requires metrically scaled data. In Sect. 2.3.3.2, the Pearson correlation coefficient matrix demonstrated that Refinitiv, ISS ESG, and S&P exhibit the closest relationships among their ESG ratings (see Fig. 2.11). As metrically scaled data are needed, their ratings were min–max normalized on a scale from 0 to 1 by applying the min–max formula described in Sect. 2.3.3.1.

For 543 out of the 600 companies, all three ESG rating providers offer ESG ratings. The analysis was conducted in R and yielded six ICC types: ICC1, ICC2, and ICC3 with corresponding K values. This aligns with the terminology of "raters" and "judges" in Shrout and Fleiss (1979). In this study, the ESG rating providers are the raters, and their ESG ratings are the judges. This framework was adopted in the present study of ESG rating providers to derive a decision tree for selecting between ICC(1, 1)/ICC(1, k), ICC(2, 1)/ICC(2, k), and ICC(3, 1)/ICC(3, k); this is articulated in Fig. 2.14.

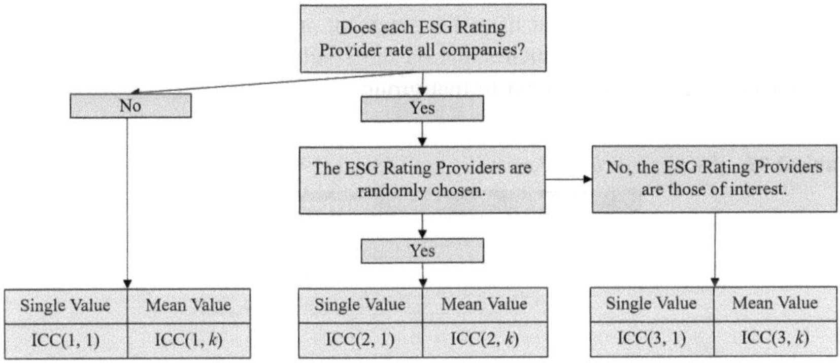

Fig. 2.14 ICC Decision Tree. (Note: Own illustration, inspired by Shrout and Fleiss (1979, p. 423 ff.))

Following the decision tree in Fig. 2.14 and the method in Shrout and Fleiss (1979), ICC3 is most appropriate. The ESG rating providers assessed all 543 companies, and the providers were selected intentionally rather than randomly. The scores are single values; hence, ICC(3,1) is applicable.

ICC3 can be expressed as follows:

$$ICC(3, 1) = \frac{BMS - EMS}{BMS + (k - 1)EMS}, \tag{2.5}$$

where *BMS* is the between-subject mean square, which assesses the extent to which the ESG ratings provided by the three providers vary across the 543 companies. The error mean square (*EMS*) measures the variation in a company's ESG ratings across the three data providers. It encompasses random error and systematic differences not accounted for by the ESG rating providers. k denotes the number of raters (i.e., the ESG rating providers).

This formula produces an ICC3 value of 0.51 with a corresponding p-value of 6.9e-89 and a lower bound of 0.462. The remarkably low p-value indicates that there is strong evidence to reject the null hypothesis that there is no agreement among the ESG rating providers. The lower bound of 0.462 signifies that, with 95% confidence, the ICC is at least 0.462. Following the ICC classifications of Cicchetti (1994) and Koo and Li (2016), which are reported in Table 2.13 and Table 2.14 respectively, an ICC3 value of 0.51 indicates moderate inter-rater agreement. This indicates that there is agreement among the raters in this group of three rating providers, which supports the results of the Pearson correlation coefficients of each combination in that group.

Table 2.13 ICC Classification According to Cicchetti (1994)

ICC	Interpretation
<0.4	Poor agreement
0.4–0.59	Moderate agreement
0.6–0.74	Good agreement
≥0.75	Excellent agreement

Table 2.14 ICC Classification According to Koo and Li (2016)

ICC	Interpretation
<0.5	Poor agreement
0.5–0.75	Moderate agreement
0.75–0.9	Good agreement
>0.9	Excellent agreement

The examples of LVMH Moet Hennessy Louis Vuitton, Nestle SA, and Deutsche Telekom (Figs. 2.15–2.17) demonstrate situations that might be confronted by an ESG investor. There are varying levels of agreement among the ESG ratings of different providers. The ratings have been adjusted so that higher ratings consistently reflect better ESG performance, aligning with the scale used by other prominent ESG rating providers.

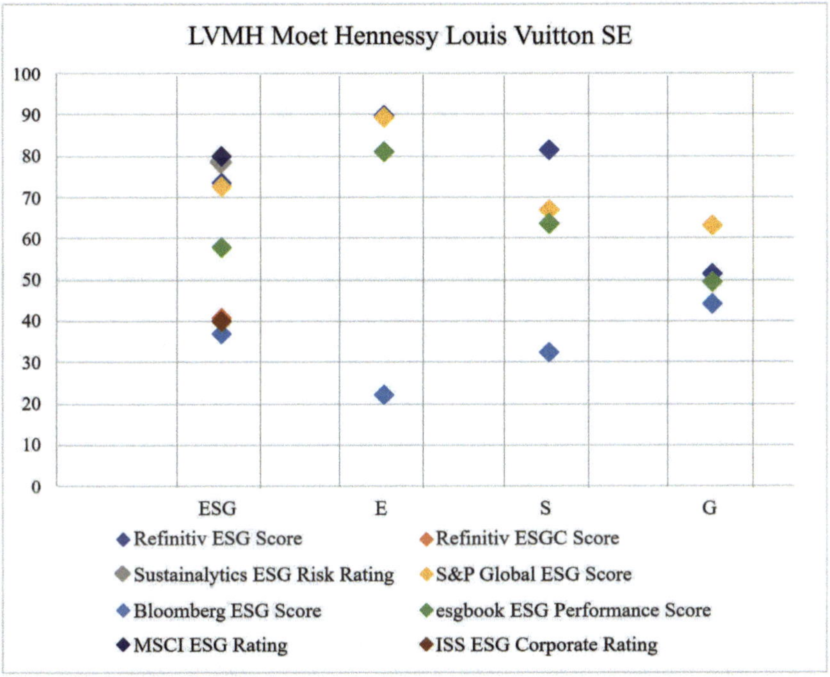

Fig. 2.15 ESG Scores and Ratings for LVMH Moet Hennessy Louis Vuitton SE as of 10.02.2023. (Note: Includes combined and dimension-specific ratings. Own illustration)

2.3.4 Conclusion and Implications

The diverse methodologies of ESG rating providers were elaborated in the preceding sections. ESG, with its three dimensions and numerous data points, can result in different investment approaches (Sect. 2.1.3). While the exclusionary investor may exclude stocks identified through supplementary information, other ESG investors who have more sophisticated approaches and pursue at least ESG inclusion require a more thorough analysis and may employ ESG ratings to ensure that investments meet a specified threshold for overall ESG performance. In this context, ESG rating providers can be beneficial; however, they should be used with cautioun. ESG rating providers have developed various models for conceptualizing corporate ESG performance. The two leading methods are ESG-performance rating, which focuses on how companies try to do good, and ESG

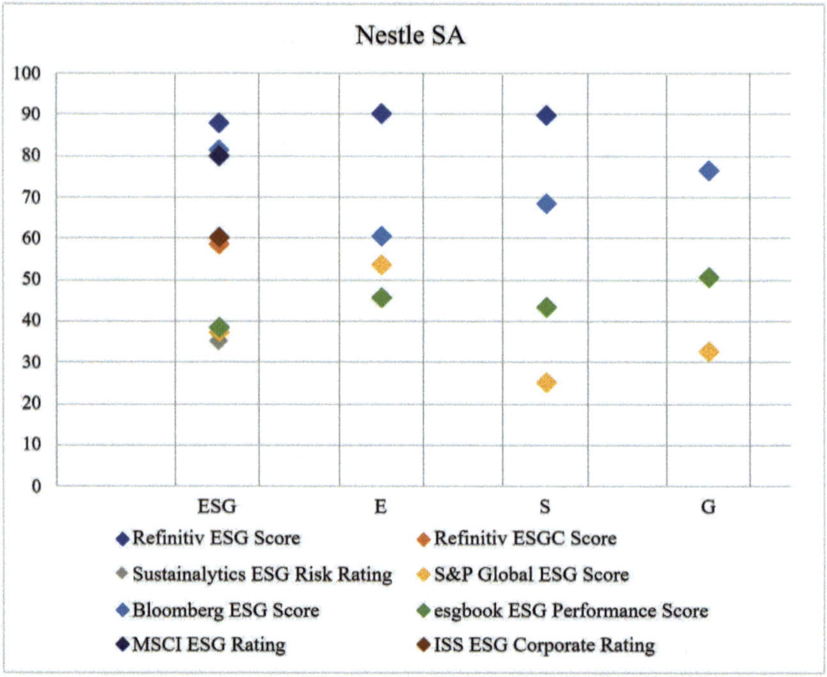

Fig. 2.16 ESG Scores and Ratings for Nestle SA as of 10.02.2023. (Note: Includes combined and dimension-specific ratings. Own illustration)

risk rating, which focuses on risks emerging due to ESG factors. Doing good and avoiding harm are not mirror images of each other; by doing good, companies do not necessarily avoid harm to their business. The differences between these perspectives are not sufficiently emphasized in current research.

The existence of two fundamentally different methods for evaluating companies' ESG commitments is not the only issue. The methods' scope and weights also vary, which can result in widely divergent ratings. The often-present sector bias also hinders investors in making cross-sectoral comparisons. Many ratings are determined based on industry benchmarks. If the ESG rating provider's scope broadens, it may affect other ratings, even without changes in the underlying data points. The expectation of a low to mid correlation has been verified. Considering the increasing amount of data and weighting options available ESG rating providers, it is highly likely that this will stay the case in the future.

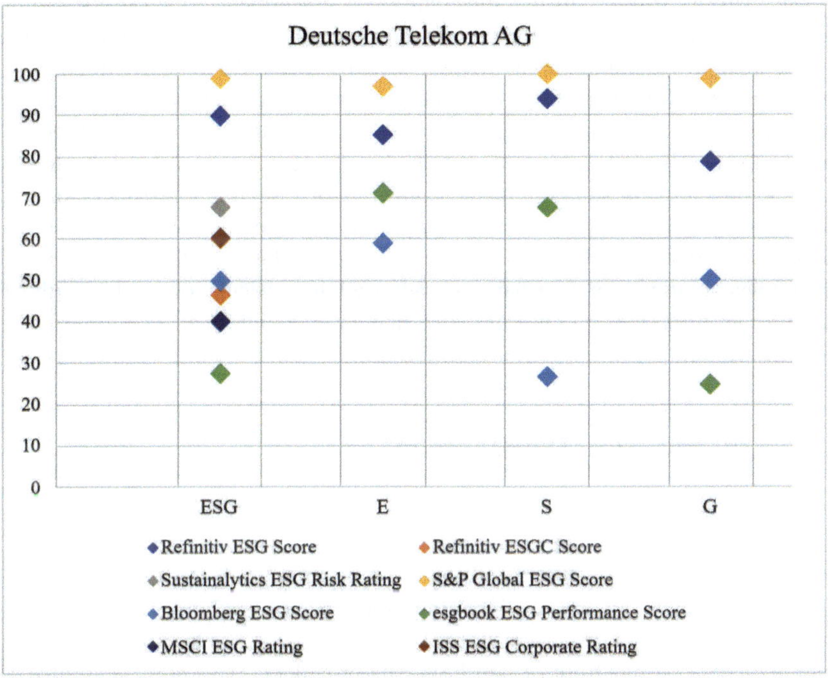

Fig. 2.17 ESG Scores and Ratings for Deutsche Telekom AG as of 10.02.2023. (Note: Includes combined and dimension-specific ratings. Own illustration)

Where ESG ratings are a part of the investment process, investors should determine their preferred methodology as the basis for choosing an ESG data provider; in this way, they can avoid confusion like that seen in the banking sector example or the examples discussed in Sect. 2.3.3.5 (see Figs. 2.15–2.17). Without sufficient information explaining the ratings, their meaning is not clear.[10]

[10] In February 2024, the European Parliament reached a political agreement to regulate ESG rating providers, with the primary objective of enhancing the governance and transparency of their rating methodologies. The agreement mandates various transparency requirements and requires the disaggregation of the E, S, and G dimensions. Additionally, it introduces crucial provisions to mitigate conflicts of interest, including the compulsory separation of ESG rating activities from consulting, audit, and credit rating activities. Anticipated benefits include increased correlation among ESG rating providers and enhanced trust in the reliability of ESG ratings. With regard to ESG investors, possible challenges include the ongoing threat

The analysis also reveals that the controversy assessment, which is not part of all methodologies, might be done by investors themselves. Also, if controversies are included in the rating but an investor would evaluate the situation differently, the controversy weighting—like other factors—is also subjective. It is worth noting that if an investor favors a particular ESG data provider and uses their ratings in investment decision-making, they bear the risk that the provider will change their methodology. In addition, the consolidation of ESG rating providers, particularly through M&As, has led to changes in their methodologies and thus in the ratings provided. In Sect. 2.3.1, Figure 2.8 shows industry M&As over the last several years; rating providers have also adjusted their calculation models without being involved in M&As. Overall, these findings highlight that investors should exercise caution when relying on ESG ratings.

2.4 Proposition Development

The preceding discussion has shown one thing: the question of whether ESG investing comes at the cost of returns cannot be categorically answered with a yes or no. The concept of ESG investing is too broad and subjectively determined. The SLR revealed a neutral to slight outperformance of ESG investing. However, most studies in the literature considered ESG funds, ESG indices, or companies with high ESG ratings from certain ESG data providers. The results were mixed. Sect. 2.3.4 indicates that ESG ratings have a sector bias, which means the final combined ESG rating is also influenced by the scope of companies analyzed by the providers. This is one of the reasons why the ratings exhibit only moderate agreement; additionally, investors carry the risk that ESG data providers may change their methodologies. The various indices agree to exclude certain companies due to their particular business dealings or their violation of the UN Global Compact. An investor who follows this approach and applies ESG exclusions during the investment process omits companies classified as NSRI, which may have nevertheless exceeded a performance benchmark, such as the STOXX Europe 600 Equal Weight Index. Based on this analysis, Hypothesis I is as follows:

of methodological changes impacting ratings and the impact of further regulatory changes. Another challenge is the potential loss of independence as a result of increased regulatory oversight (European Parliament, 2024).

H I) By excluding companies classified as NSRI, exclusionary ESG investors do not limit their investment universe and omit companies that outperform a benchmark, such as the STOXX Europe 600 Equal Weight Index.

An ESG investor employing an ESG inclusion approach incorporates ESG considerations when assessing a company's ESG profile. This may involve setting predefined ESG rating thresholds and selectively investing in companies that meet these criteria. Additionally, by generally avoiding companies that have faced ESG controversies in the past, the investor may avoid investing in companies that pose financial and reputational risks, including potential legal issues, regulatory penalties, and public backlash. Avoiding such companies may minimize unforeseen risks and avoid underperformance. Based on the above, Hypothesis II is proposed as follows:

H II)By avoiding companies that have faced ESG controversies, investors can avoid underperformance.

For example, Sect. 1.1 has demonstrated that companies doing good in fields that are environmentally important to the sector may be safe from or better prepared for new regulatory requirements. Additionally, companies with a stronger ESG profile tend to have access to cheaper capital. ESG rating providers may not give sufficient weight to crucial metrics among the many that they consider. Companies that treat their employees well (see footnote 5) may attract more talent, have better working conditions, and experience less knowledge loss; the characteristics of a good working environment are covered by certain social and governance metrics.[11]

An opportunity could be that the company has a competitive advantage, such as a production process that uses fewer energy resources than its competitors. Risks can be avoided at the micro level by evaluating the business model in light of ESG factors at the company level. This study has shown that ESG investing is highly subjective. However, the non-correlation and high divergence among

---

[11] The importance of human capital and its impact on productivity and innovation have also been suggested by the Solow growth model, enhanced with human capital by the authors of "A Contribution to the empirics of economic Growth" in 1992 (Mankiw et al., 1992). Dornbusch et al. (2018) added "H" for human capital to the production function; they also suggest that in industrialized countries, the skills and talents of workers are more critical than mere raw labor. They argue that an organization can enhance its skill base through investments in human capital, such as education and training, similar to how physical capital is augmented through investment. This can be seen in the S&P 500. The share of intangible asset market value was 17% in 1975 and 90% in 2020; the share of intangible assets of the S&P Europe 350 was 74% in 2020 according to Ocean Tomo (2022).

the various rating providers show that there is no agreement on the scope and weighting of ESG criteria and their metrics.

The literature review has shown that some ESG indices or ratings used in investment strategies have resulted in returns over the benchmark. If the providers' methodologies are disregarded and the focus is on the metrics, there might be some that generate outperformance. This is how an ESG investor acts in the ESG inclusion stage of decision-making. It is certain that the more barriers an ESG investor includes in their metrics, the narrower their investment universe becomes. Nevertheless, if the ESG investor selects ESG metrics that are related to company success more generally (i.e., serving as proxies for a high-performing company) and thus may generate alpha, the investor may be able to separate the wheat from the chaff. Hypothesis III is therefore as follows:

H III) Certain ESG metrics are signals for financial returns.

Methodology and Data Analysis 3

3.1 Data Collection

As in Sect. 2.3.3, the statistical analyses were conducted using the R programming language (version 4.2.2), its graphical user interface RStudio (version 2023.12.1, build 402), and various R libraries. Straightforward calculations and basic data organization were performed using Microsoft Excel. The data collection process was carried out using Refinitiv Eikon, which offers multiple ESG metrics. The scope was expanded beyond the 600 companies comprising the STOXX Europe 600 for a thorough analysis. All publicly listed companies headquartered in Europe were included, as identified through the Eikon Refinitiv screening process. This substantially broadened dataset allows for a more comprehensive analysis. In total, data were retrieved for 843 metrics (see Table 3.1) from 11,035 companies located in 45 different European countries from Refinitiv Eikon and exported to Excel. Table 3.2 shows the number of companies by sector. Figure 3.1 displays the number of listed companies in the top 10 countries. The ESG data were taken for the period from 2011 to 2021, and the total annual returns were taken for each following year, from 2012 to 2022. The total returns include both the price change and the dividends received. The sector classification follows the Refinitiv Business Classification. Due to the limited number of companies within the academic and educational services and government activity sectors, these were omitted from the following analysis. The final dataset includes 11,002 companies, with no changes to the number of represented countries (45).

Supplementary Information The online version contains supplementary material available at https://doi.org/10.1007/978-3-658-49789-7_3.

A. Schleipfer, *The Value of ESG Metrics in the Investment Process*,
https://doi.org/10.1007/978-3-658-49789-7_3

Table 3.1 Retrieved Numerical and Binary Metrics by Dimension

Dimension	Environmental	Social	Governance
Number of Metrics	437	248	158

Table 3.2 Number of Companies by Sector

Refinitiv Business Classification	Number of Companies
Academic and Educational Services	30
Basic Materials	830
Consumer Cyclicals	1,670
Consumer Non-Cyclicals	809
Energy	427
Financial	1,821
Government Activity	3
Healthcare	836
Industrial	2,043
Real Estate	813
Technology	1,379
Utilities	374

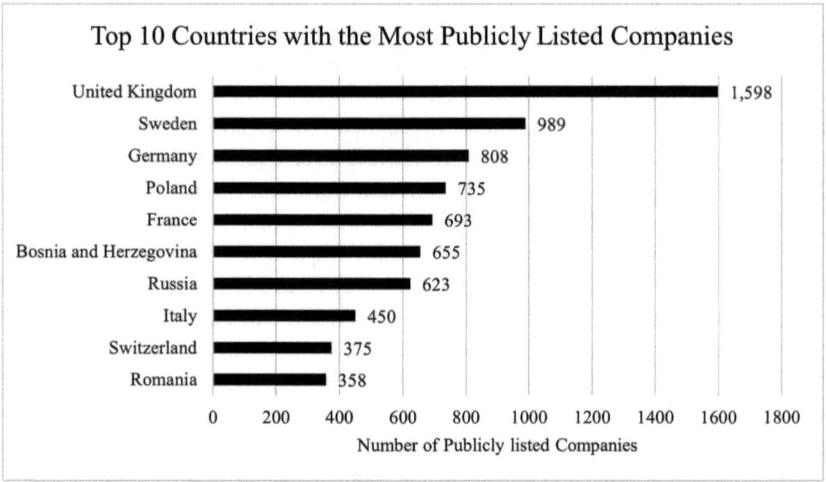

Fig. 3.1 Top 10 Countries with Publicly Listed Companies Headquartered in Europe During the Observation Period. (Note: Own illustration)

For consistency, the STOXX Europe 600 Equal Weight Net Return Index (SXXEWR) serves as the benchmark, as it includes both the price change and the dividends received. For simplicity, it will hereafter be referred to as the STOXX Europe 600 Equal Weight NR Index, unless otherwise specified.

3.2 Hypothesis I: ESG Exclusion

Hypothesis I: By excluding companies classified as NSRI, exclusionary ESG investors do not limit the investment universe and omit companies that outperform a benchmark, such as the STOXX Europe 600 Equal Weight NR Index.

3.2.1 Methodology and Portfolio Construction

Hypothesis I was tested using data for companies typically excluded by SRI and ESG indices as analyzed in Sect. 2.1.1 and presented in Appendix A (ESM), Table A1. The analyzed dataset encompasses the required information on whether a company is involved in specific businesses, represented as binary yes/no data. This information was taken to determine if a company belongs to a sector typically excluded by SRI and ESG indices. For some metrics, information was only available after 2017; before this time, they were assigned a null value rather than being designated as "true" or "false." I assumed that these metrics with null values were true or false depending on what they showed prior to 2017. The "UN Global Compact Violation Flag" metric assesses whether companies have violated any of the principles of the UN Global Compact. For companies with a null value, this has been assumed to be false.

Table A1 shows that some indices have imposed extensive sectoral exclusions. Therefore, companies were separated into two groups for this analysis: companies involved in business activities excluded by at least three indices and companies involved in business activities excluded by at least one index (see Sect. 2.1.1). Companies that violate the 10 principles of the UN Global Compact, which constitutes general failure, are categorized separately into a third group.

The metrics in the dataset are more detailed, so they have been assigned to the NSRI category. Table 3.3 shows the three groups along with the specified metrics and the corresponding penalized sectors.

Table 3.3 Metrics Assigned to NSRI Categories Excluded by ESG Indices

Metric	NSRI Category		
Adult Entertainment Producer	Adult Entertainment	Group 1	Group 2
Pornography			
Alcohol Producer	Alcohol		
Alcohol			
Chemical or Biological Weapons	Controversial Weapons		
Nuclear Weapons			
Cluster Munitions			
Military Weapons or Personnel	Conventional Weapons		
Firearms Producer			
Firearms			
Gambling Operator and Producer	Gambling		
Gambling			
Nuclear Power Generation	Nuclear Power		
Uranium Mining and Processing			
Thermal Coal Producer	Thermal Coal		
Thermal Coal-Fired Power Generation			
Tobacco Producer	Tobacco		
Tobacco			
Arctic Oil Producer	Unconventional Oil and Gas		
Oil Sands Producer			
Armaments	Abortion and Contraception		
Contraceptives			
Abortifacients			
Animal Testing	Animal Testing		
Animal Testing Cosmetics			
GMO Products	Genetically Modified Organisms		
Oil and Gas Producer	Oil and Gas		
Oil and Gas Processing, Transportation and Distribution			
Oil and Gas-Fired Power Generation			
Oilfield Services			
Embryonic Stem Cell Research	Stem Cell Research		
UN Global Compact Flag	UN Global Compact Violators	Group 3	

Three portfolios were built and observed over the period from 2013 to 2022. The portfolios for each group were constructed using the prepared dataset in Sect. 3.1. The returns of Group 1 companies involved in at least one of the penalized categories were identified for each year from 2012 to 2021. The portfolio was reconstructed prior to the first trading day of each year. The data reported in the prior year were decisive in determining whether a company was qualified to join the portfolio. All positions were equally weighted, which is a common approach in research and can be justified by the elimination of market risk due to the number of positions; this is also known as naïve portfolio construction (Bloomfield et al., 1977; DeMiguel et al., 2009). In composing the portfolio, a market capitalization threshold of equal to or greater than EUR 0.5 billion was set following the methodology of the STOXX Europe 600 index, which includes the 600 largest companies and reflects the free-float market capitalization of each sector (Deutsche Boerse Group, 2024). Thus, in addition to so-called micro-cap companies, which are characterized by their lack of liquidity and wide bid–ask spread, small-cap companies were omitted.

The following formula was applied to calculate the return for each year:

$$R_{it} = \prod\nolimits_{t=1}^{n} \left(1 + BI_{c,\,t-1}\right) - 1, \tag{3.1}$$

where R_{it} is the return of portfolio i in period t and $BI_{c,t-1}$ is a binary variable indicating the involvement in non-socially responsible business activities in period t-1 for company c. The annualized rate of return is the compound annual growth rate (CAGR), calculated as follows:

$$CAGR = (\prod\nolimits_{t=1}^{n} (1 + R_{it}))^{\frac{1}{n}} - 1, \tag{3.2}$$

The ex post annualized Sharpe ratios are calculated using monthly returns to set the portfolio returns in relation to their risk. This makes it possible to compare them to the respective regional index benchmarks, such as the STOXX Europe 600 Equal Weight NR Index. The Sharpe ratio is a metric for evaluating a portfolio's performance in relation to its risk level. It is calculated by dividing the portfolio's excess return (relative to the risk-free rate) by its standard deviation. This provides insight into how well an investment has performed in light of the risk taken. This study has taken into account the risk-free rate represented by the monthly return on German government bonds. There are various opinions in the literature regarding how the Sharpe ratio should be interpreted, and this also depends on the asset type considered. According to Pav (2021), a Sharpe ratio above $0.5yr^{-\frac{1}{2}}$ is considered good, and a Sharpe ratio above $1yr^{-\frac{1}{2}}$ is considered very good. The formula for the annualized Sharpe ratio is as follows:

$$SharpeRatio = \frac{R_p - R_f}{\sigma_p}\sqrt{12}, \tag{3.3}$$

where R_p is the average monthly return of the portfolio, R_f is the risk-free rate of return, and σ_p is the standard deviation of the portfolio's excess return.

The Sharpe ratio is often criticized because it does not differentiate between upside and downside volatility. High outlier returns have been found to elevate the value of the denominator (standard deviation) more significantly than the numerator, leading to a reduction in the ratio value. The Sortino ratio is a modification of the Sharpe ratio that uses the downside instead of standard deviation to measure risk. It specifically focuses on returns below a required rate of return, which here is the risk-free rate represented by the monthly returns of German bonds. Markowitz acknowledged when developing the modern portfolio theory that for investors, only downside deviation matters, and it is more suitable as a measure of risk than standard deviation. Due to computational impracticality at the time when Markowitz was developing his theory, he used variance. The Sortino ratio is ideal for cross-portfolio and cross-strategy comparisons, with a higher ratio indicating superior risk-adjusted performance (Schulmerich et al., 2015). Given the wide popularity and widespread use of both ratios in the literature, this study calculates both. The annualized Sortino ratio is calculated as follows:

$$SortinoRatio = \frac{R_p - R_f}{\sigma_d}\sqrt{12}, \tag{3.4}$$

where σ_d is the downside deviation of the excess returns.

This downside deviation is calculated as follows:

$$DownsideDeviation = \sqrt{\frac{\sum_{t=1}^{n}(\min(R_t - R_f))^2}{n}}, \tag{3.5}$$

where R_t is the return of the portfolio in month t and n is the number of periods.

3.2.2 Results and Research Findings

The NSRI portfolios generated higher returns than the STOXX Europe 600 Equal Weight NR Index during the period from 2013 to 2022. The Group 1 portfolio, which only considers companies involved in businesses excluded by at least three of the indices considered, had a total return of 161.74% after 10 years, which is an annualized rate of return of 10.10% (see Table 3.4).

Group 2, which encompasses all business sectors, had a total return of 167.32% and a similar annualized rate of return of 10.33% (see Table 3.5).

Table 3.4 Yearly Returns of Group 1 Companies

Group 1					
Year	**2013**	**2014**	**2015**	**2016**	**2017**
Return	30.54%	9.51%	15.45%	10.37%	21.21%
Companies	102	105	105	109	115
Year	**2018**	**2019**	**2020**	**2021**	**2022**
Return	-8.73%	23.60%	0.26%	18.47%	-11.53%
Companies	120	120	124	129	130

Table 3.5 Yearly Returns of Group 2 Companies

Group 2					
Year	**2013**	**2014**	**2015**	**2016**	**2017**
Return	29.38%	6.56%	16.40%	10.93%	19.86%
Companies	277	289	299	322	332
Year	**2018**	**2019**	**2020**	**2021**	**2022**
Return	-9.09%	26.36%	4.76%	18.31%	-11.99%
Companies	347	347	359	372	372

Companies that have violated the UN Global Compact Principles are placed in Group 3. This portfolio had returns of 85.79%, which is equal to an annualized rate of return of 6.39% (see Table 3.6).

Table 3.6 Yearly Returns of Group 3 Companies

Group 3					
Year	**2013**	**2014**	**2015**	**2016**	**2017**
Return	23.42%	0.16%	4.52%	12.35%	13.52%
Companies	91	77	78	61	78
Year	**2018**	**2019**	**2020**	**2021**	**2022**
Return	-15.21%	17.08%	-8.46%	25.30%	-0.98%
Companies	78	98	97	100	81

The STOXX Europe 600 Equal Weight NR Index returned 93.96% over the same period, with an annualized rate of return of 6.85% (see Table 3.7).

All groups exhibited better performance from 2013 to 2022 than the STOXX Europe 600 Equal Weight NR Index, except the group of companies that violated the UN Global Compact. The exclusion of sectors classified as NSRI is

Table 3.7 Yearly Returns of the STOXX Europe 600 Equal Weight Net Return Index

STOXX Europe 600 Equal Weight Index (SXXEWR)					
Year	**2013**	**2014**	**2015**	**2016**	**2017**
Return	20.85%	7.05%	14.00%	1.59%	14.47%
Companies	600	600	600	600	600
Year	**2018**	**2019**	**2020**	**2021**	**2022**
Return	-11.94%	28.06%	1.71%	21.74%	-19.02%
Companies	600	600	600	600	600

effectively an exclusion of stocks that tend to perform better on average than the benchmark. An ESG investor who excludes NSRI companies would have limited their investment universe to companies that outperformed the benchmark, even though it is crucial to recognize that their investment universe remains substantial. Excluding companies that have violated the UN Global Compact effectively removes those that underperformed relative to the benchmark.

The two risk ratios, the Sharpe and Sortino ratios (see Tables 3.8 and 3.9), can provide insights that go beyond simple returns.

Table 3.8 Sharpe Ratios of the Three Portfolios and the Benchmark

	Portfolio Group 1	Portfolio Group 2	Portfolio Group 3	STOXX Europe 600 Equal Weight Index
2Y Sharpe Ratio	1.79	1.78	0.99	1.36
5Y Sharpe Ratio	1.55	1.49	0.88	0.92
10Y Sharpe Ratio	0.72	0.76	0.45	0.48

Table 3.9 Sortino Ratios of the Three Portfolios and the Benchmark

	Portfolio Group 1	Portfolio Group 2	Portfolio Group 3	STOXX Europe 600 Equal Weight Index
2Y Sortino Ratio	5.18	4.97	2.26	2.84
5Y Sortino Ratio	3.37	2.95	1.74	1.51
10Y Sortino Ratio	1.13	1.20	0.69	0.70

Due to their superior returns in comparison to the STOXX Europe 600 Equal Weight NR Index, especially over a longer period, it is not surprising that the two portfolios demonstrate markedly better Sharpe and Sortino ratios after each calculated period. Hypothesis I was that omitting NSRI companies does not limit the investing universe by excluding companies with above-average performance. However, the results of this study do not support this hypothesis.

3.3 Hypothesis II: ESG Inclusion

Hypothesis II: The avoidance of companies with ESG controversies avoids underperformance.

3.3.1 Methodology and Portfolio Construction

Refinitiv considers 55 metrics across the three ESG dimensions that reflect the various controversies a company might have faced during the year. These metrics either provide a number or record a response of true if the company has been in the media spotlight and linked to particular controversies (Refinitiv Eikon, 2022). The 55 metrics were combined into a single characterization variable, which is "true" if observations have been recorded and "false" if there were no controversies recorded. The idea here is that a company's ESG violation, which covers all types of controversies, is a high-level ESG risk for that company, and it should thus be avoided during portfolio construction. To obtain as compelling evidence as possible, I compare two portfolios from each sector, namely *ESG_contro_true* and *ESG_contro_false*. Being associated with one controversy in the year before the portfolio was built (*t*-1) classified a company as *contro_true,* and it was then put into the portfolio *ESG_contro_true* on January 1 of year *t*.

As in Hypothesis I, the portfolios were compiled prior to the first trading day of each year. Two approaches have been followed in the further analysis. The first is that the investment should be excluded for the following year, and the second is that it should be excluded for the next two years. The second approach should mitigate the ambiguity in the data related to whether a controversy in the previous year happened just before or after the portfolios were composed. I have not extended the analysis beyond two years, as the significance of the controversy and its potential to be resolved could not be measured based on the data available. All other companies were placed into *ESG_contro_false*. There was no further weighting of positions within a portfolio; they were equally weighted. A market capitalization threshold of EUR 0.3 billion was predefined; this is lower than the level set for the investigation of Hypothesis I. This adjustment was made as the STOXX Europe 600 Equal Weight NR Index was not utilized as a benchmark.

The EUR 0.3 billion threshold was set to exclude companies lacking trading volume and in possible financial distress. Such companies may be more vulnerable to price volatility as small trading volumes lead to significant price swings. Financially distressed companies were excluded as news about their financial health is the predominant investment driver. The market capitalization threshold must be exceeded on January 1 each year. This analysis also employs the dataset described in Sect. 3.1, covering the data reported on the final day of the years from 2011 to 2021, which allows for the initial portfolio built on January 1, 2013, to have the necessary two years of data to draw on.

A benchmark portfolio against which the "ESG-controversy" portfolios can be measured was constructed using companies that are in the same sector but did not face any controversies. The STOXX Europe 600 Equal Weight NR Index is not appropriate for the sector-wise comparison since it includes many sectors. Due to a lack of companies that faced controversies, the real estate sector was omitted (Table 3.10).

Table 3.10 Controversies Across Sectors by ESG Dimension

			Allocation of Controversies		
Sector	Observations	Controversies	E	S	G
Basic Materials	5,196	223 (4.29%)	16.99%	77.61%	5.41%
Consumer Cyclicals	9,666	303 (3.13%)	10.48%	69.89%	19.62%
Consumer Non-Cyclicals	4,261	197 (4.62%)	4.78%	81.74%	13.48%
Industrial	11,060	384 (34.72%)	1.98%	90.86%	7.16%
Energy	3,017	186 (6.17%)	15.95%	75.86%	8.19%
Financial	11,606	394 (3.39%)	1.28%	80.77%	17.95%
Healthcare	5,467	161 (2.94%)	6.97%	76.62%	16.42%
Real Estate	4,951	10 (0.20%)	0.00%	80.00%	20.0%
Technology	8,980	231 (25.72%)	0.40%	86.06%	13.55%
Utilities	2,154	116 (5.39%)	12.31%	81.54%	6.15%

3.3.2 Results and Research Findings

The single characterization variable covers several controversy types. Governance controversies, such as accounting or management controversies, may prevent a traditional investor from investing in a company due to a general lack of trust. This is a reminder that governance factors have long been relevant. The ESG inclusionary investor would additionally consider environmental and social controversies. Using the ESG lens, an investor would focus on the effects of these controversies on the company's anticipated performance; for example, there might be financial pressure resulting from fines and customer boycotts or challenges in recruiting new talent due to a tarnished reputation among potential employees. For this type of ESG investor, a company's fundamental financial profile would be secondary in their investment decision-making. Therefore, proxies such as financial or market capitalization have been omitted.

The average annualized return of the *ESG_contro_true* portfolios, as shown in Fig. 3.2, was lower than the benchmark portfolios across all sectors when controversy was avoided in the next year. Where further controversy was avoided for the two years following the initial event, the *ESG_contro_true* portfolios showed poor performance across all sectors except for energy. For both the one-year and the two-year observation periods, the annual average return was lower than the average return of the three NSRI portfolio groups (see Sect. 3.2.2). The results also show that companies in the *ESG_contro_true* portfolios that were in the technology and healthcare sectors performed significantly worse than those in other sectors; the financial and industrial sectors delivered the next worst performance. Another interesting finding is that this exclusionary approach excluded companies that violated the UN Global Compact Principles. These principles are designed to uphold fundamental responsibilities and are reflected in the ESG controversy metrics.

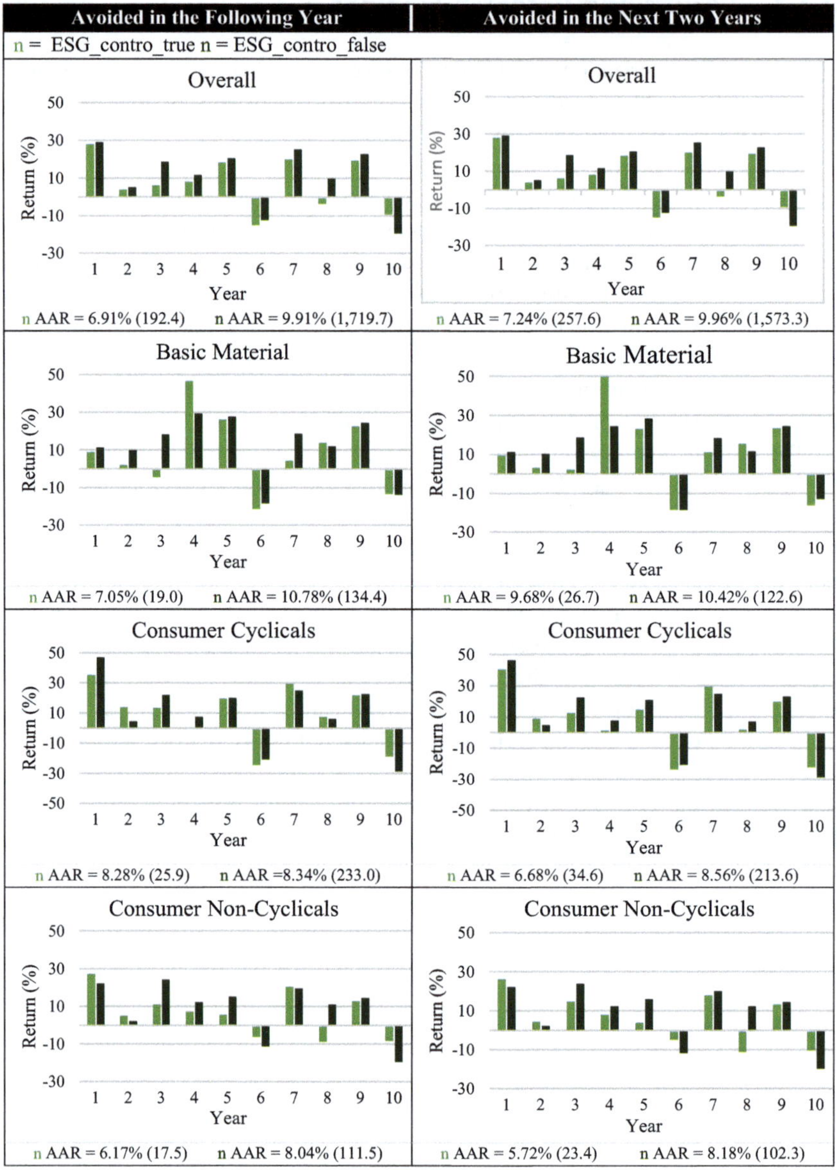

Fig. 3.2 Average Annual Returns for ESG_contro_true and ESG_contro_false in 2013–2022. (Note: Own illustration. Yearly average number of stocks in the portfolio in brackets)

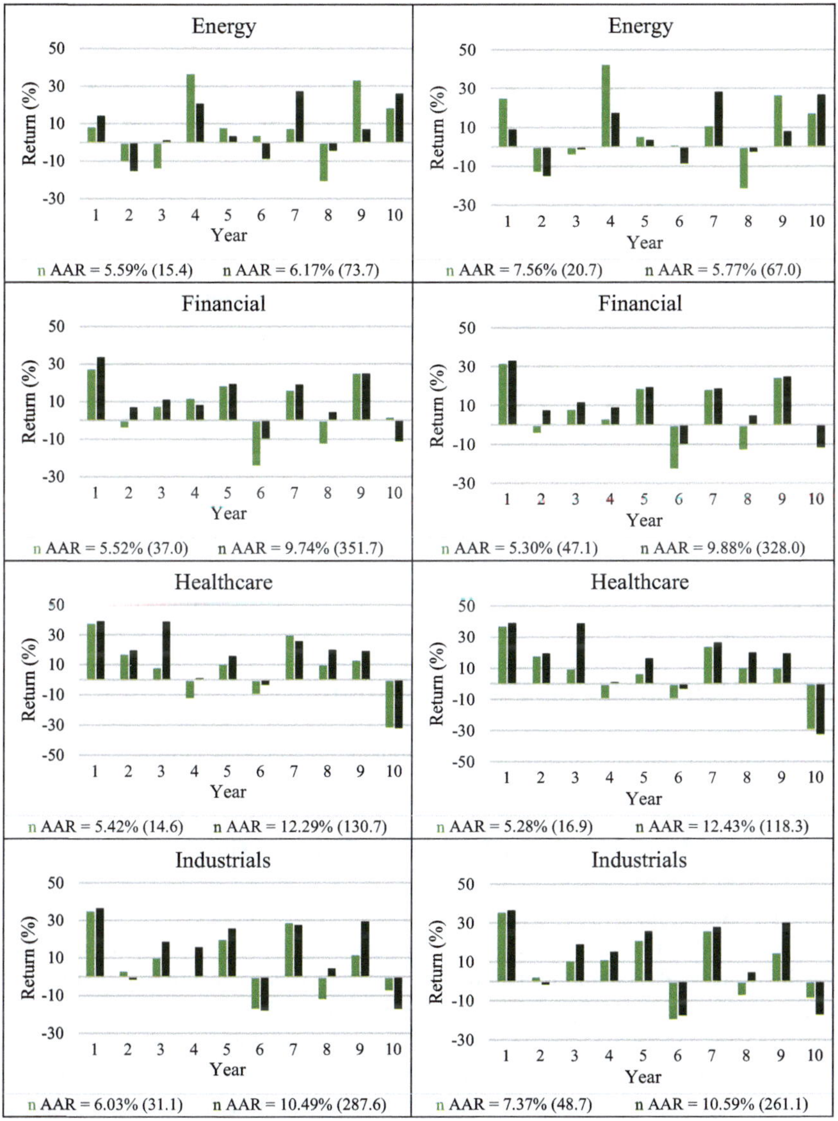

Fig. 3.2 (continued)

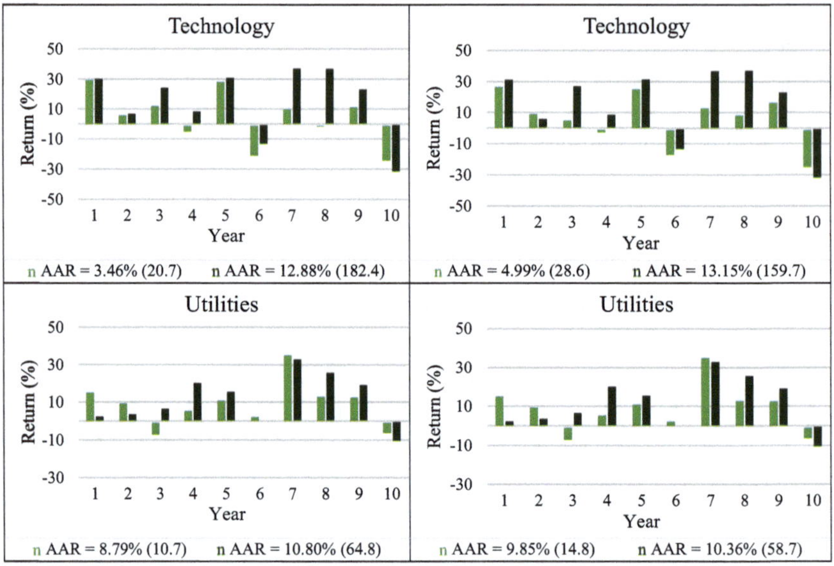

Fig. 3.2 (continued)

3.4 Hypothesis III: ESG Integration

Hypothesis III: Certain ESG metrics are signals for financial returns.

3.4.1 Methodology and Portfolio Construction

Testing this hypothesis shows if there are metrics that can be connected to alpha. The dataset described in Sect. 3.1 was employed, and the 843 retrieved ESG metrics were analyzed and prepared. The first step was to ensure that there were sufficient data available for all sectors. Metrics reported by fewer than 30 companies per year for each sector or that did not span a minimum of five years were excluded from the analysis unless the metric in question was sector-specific. In the next step, metrics without meaningful context, such as total amounts, were removed, including "board size," "board size more ten less eight," and "number of board meetings." This process resulted in 207 metrics remaining, which were then categorized according to their nature into numerical and binary types (see Appendix A (ESM), Tables A8–A10). Table 3.11 shows the distribution of numerical and binary metrics across ESG dimensions.

Table 3.11 Distribution of Numerical and Binary Metrics Across ESG Dimensions

Environmental		Social		Governance	
Numerical	Binary	Numerical	Binary	Numerical	Binary
29	10	22	48	32	66

Next, two portfolios were constructed for each metric, one labeled *ESG_good* and the other *ESG_bad.* For numerical metrics, the "good" portfolio consisted of companies with the top 10 values for the metric in question, and the "bad" portfolio comprised companies with the bottom 10 values. Companies that had the same values recorded as a company ranked in the top or bottom 10 were also included in the portfolio. For binary metrics, all those companies with metrics marked as either true or false were placed in their respective portfolios. Null values were omitted in all cases. No additional variables were incorporated, highlighting a primary emphasis on the ESG metrics. I argued that ESG metrics and financial returns are not disparate factors; rather, as EU regulators argue, ESG metrics serve as reliable indicators of sound business practices and effective risk management, thereby contributing to superior financial performance. A threshold market capitalization of EUR 0.25 billion was set to have as much data as possible while ensuring that no companies facing financial distress were included.

The portfolios were composed annually on January 1 based on the data reported in the preceding year, with each position equally weighted. This process was automated using R (version 4.2.2), RStudio (version 2023.12.1, build 402), and the R package dplyr (version 1.1.0) (see Appendix B (ESM)). This resulted in 416 portfolios for each of the 10 sectors, which were exported from R and further analyzed in Microsoft Excel (365, version 2023).

The return was calculated for the observation year only if at least 20 companies were identified—10 for the top and 10 for the bottom portfolio. This ensured that the return for the observation year was not determined by only a few available companies. If, over the span of 10 years, fewer than 40 companies were identified and/or the available returns covered fewer than six years, the metric fell out of scope for the particular sector. Metrics that were de-scoped for all sectors during the cleansing process were subsequently removed; this resulted in 119 remaining metrics.

Each portfolio included a minimum of 10 equally weighted companies. Therefore, the Sharpe and Sortino ratios provide an indicative measure of the risk-adjusted portfolio performance by also considering the volatility experienced over time. This is particularly insightful for those portfolios that exhibited remarkable outperformance.

3.4.2 Results and Research Findings

In Appendix A of the ESM, Tables A11 and A12 set out the returns of the various portfolios. For clarity, the *ESG_good* portfolios are shaded using a diverging intensity scale, reflecting the performance of *ESG_good* relative to *ESG_bad* (see Table 3.12). Cells are left unshaded when the absolute difference in annualized returns between the portfolios is less than 0.5%.

Table 3.12 Shading of the Metric Return Tables

Color	Interpretation
	No difference (|absolute difference| <0.5%)
	No available data
	Low positive annualized return (≤5%)
	High positive annualized return (>5%)
	Low negative annualized return (≥-5%)
	High negative annualized return (<-5%)

The analysis shows that there are metrics for which the *ESG_good* portfolios performed significantly better. Only two metrics consistently outperformed in all sectors: "anti-competition controversies bribery" and "corruption and fraud controversies." Since these are controversy metrics, Hypothesis II is supported. For Hypothesis III, further controversy-related metrics were eliminated during the data cleaning process. The findings emphasize that for investors seeking a blend of financial performance and ESG considerations, certain sector-specific metrics consistently led to outperformance. There are also *ESG_bad* portfolios that significantly outperformed *ESG_good* portfolios. This was expected, especially given that other research on the topic has not confirmed a connection between ESG ratings and financial returns. I have further analyzed and filtered for those metrics in which the *ESG_good* portfolio outperformed its *ESG_bad* counterpart by at least 3% on an annualized rate of return. This threshold was chosen to capture performance differences that are economically meaningful over time while remaining inclusive enough to reflect a broad range of relevant metrics. These metrics, along with the associated risk measurements, are presented in Appendix A (ESM), Tables A13–A22.

An important finding is that the outperforming metrics are proxies for good business practices and robust ESG risk management, with a notable dominance of Governance metrics. This may be partly due to higher data availability in the Governance domain, while Environmental and Social metrics are expected to become more reliable as data quality improves. Metrics that are particularly relevant within their respective sectors tend to outperform. For instance, in the basic materials sector, Social (S) metrics such as "lost time injury rate (employees)" and "average training hours" consistently outperformed. In the consumer cyclicals sector, "lost time injury rate (employees)" and low "turnover of employees" were key outperformers as well.

Some ESG metrics for which outperformance was recorded are associated with risks; for example, "total CO_2 equivalent emissions to revenues" and "total energy use to revenues" indicate the company's dependence on energy (costs) and the potential threat of rising CO_2 prices. Comparatively, many metrics in the financial sector indicate outperformance or do not lead to underperformance, especially Governance metrics and measures such as "ESG reporting scope". This may be a result of the lessons learned from the financial crisis of 2007–2008, leading the sector to report more data and investors to scrutinize these metrics more carefully This crisis generated increased regulatory scrutiny and a demand for greater transparency, especially in the banking sector. In addition, banks needed to rehabilitate their image as investors became more cautious. In the energy and utilities sectors, a broad range of policy-based governance metrics and a strong emphasis on environmental restoration initiatives further support the sector-specific relevance of ESG measures. The finding that sound business practices and advanced ESG risk management are present reinforces the importance of reporting company-specific ESG impacts, opportunities, and, risks, as mandated by the Corporate Sustainability Reporting Directive. Additionally, almost all *ESG_good* portfolios exhibit a lower risk profile, as evidenced by the 10-year Sharpe and Sortino ratios for these portfolios compared to the *ESG_bad* portfolios (see Appendix A (ESM), Tables A13–A22).[1]

[1] Due to limited data availability, not all metrics could be used to measure the 10-year risk-adjusted Sharpe and Sortino ratios. The numbers in parentheses state the years for which data are available.

3.5 Application of Research Findings

A further test was conducted to confirm the research findings using a potential investor's strategy combining ESG exclusion, integration, and inclusion.

As discussed in Sect. 2.1, ESG exclusion is a popular approach and has therefore been included in this investment process, even though NSRI companies from Group 1 and Group 2 exhibited better performance than the benchmark of the STOXX Europe 600 Equal Weight NR Index (Sect. 3.2). Consequently, NSRI companies belonging to Group 2 and thus belonging to Group 1 (defined with respect to Hypothesis I) were therefore excluded. Companies that violated the UN Global Compact Principles were also excluded.

Avoiding companies involved in ESG controversies in the preceding year is part of the ESG inclusion approach and has been examined in Hypothesis II. ESG controversies are recorded as risks to the investor's future financial return. Besides considering risks, the investor following an ESG inclusion approach would also have set some general ESG rating thresholds.

The various ESG metrics indicating financial returns, identified in the development of Hypothesis III, reflect sector-specific ESG attributes. For the shift from a long to a short list of potential investments, the investor would, as an integral part of the ESG inclusion process, explicitly select companies that meet predefined ESG criteria to enhance portfolio performance, as explored in Hypothesis III. To ensure comprehensive sectoral representation and a minimum of one ESG metric per sector, a threshold was applied based on the smallest observed difference in annualized returns between the ESG_good and ESG_bad portfolios. This threshold—set at 4.899%—was derived from the performance gap in the real estate sector, where the ESG_good portfolio based on renewable energy use achieved an annual return of 6.853% compared to 1.954% for the ESG_bad portfolio. This approach ensured that at least one financially meaningful ESG metric—available for a minimum of six years—was included for each sector. The ESG inclusion process also involves setting thresholds; at least half of the identified metrics must either surpass the sector's average or exhibit a positive stance from an ESG perspective. Null values were counted as a negative stance. Again, this resulted in a more limited investment portfolio in the initial years.

A market capitalization threshold of EUR 0.5 billion was applied to ensure comparability with the STOXX Europe 600 can serve as a benchmark. No further analyses were performed; the holistic ESG screening process is depicted in Fig. 3.3.

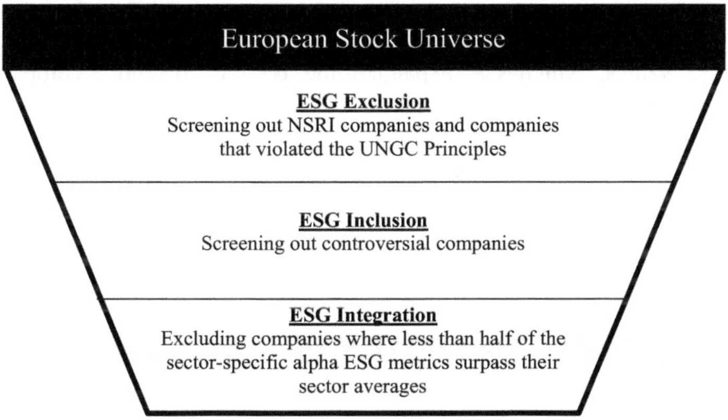

Fig. 3.3 ESG Screening Strategy. (Note: Own illustration)

The approach is also a point-based method, somewhat similar to the method for calculating the Piotroski F-score, which is calculated based on specific financial indicators to assess a company's overall financial health and value. The numerical ESG metrics were converted into binary variables and designated as "true" if they surpassed the sector's average in a positive stance. Together with the other binary ESG metrics, which were marked as true if their overall statement was positive from an ESG perspective, the company was included in the portfolio if at least half of all ESG metrics were deemed true.

For example, in the basic materials sector for which 13 ESG metrics were identified (see Sect. 3.4), nine were numerical and thus converted into binary variables. Four true/false variables were already present. Also included in the ESG portfolio were companies that had market capitalization above EUR 0.5 billion, had no controversies in the previous year, were not involved in non-social (NSRI) business activities according to Group 2, and had at least seven ESG metrics marked as true. As with the other portfolio constructions, the reporting year t was decisive for the portfolio composition on January 1 in the year $t + 1$. The stocks qualified for the ESG portfolio each year are set out in Table 3.13.

Table 3.13 Companies in the Basic Materials Sector That Qualify for the ESG Portfolio Each Year

Year	2013	2014	2015	2016	2017	2018	2019	2020	2021	2022
Companies	27	26	29	34	33	38	50	53	60	63

As previously mentioned, there has been an increase in data availability for metrics over the past years. Consequently, fewer metrics were omitted due to missing values, which has expanded the pool of potential companies as investment targets.

This process was repeated for all sectors and resulted in an ESG portfolio with the number of stocks and annual portfolio returns over the period from 2013 to 2022 reported in Table 3.14.

Table 3.14 Number of Companies Included in the ESG Portfolio Each Year and Annual Returns

Year	2013	2014	2015	2016	2017
Stocks	151	150	164	205	215
Return (%)	29.51	11.18	18.12	11.65	18.44
Year	**2018**	**2019**	**2020**	**2021**	**2022**
Stocks	260	318	416	506	626
Return (%)	−9.23	30.74	4.94	25.81	−18.35

This portfolio results in an average return of 12.28% each year and an annualized rate of return of 11.15%, which exceeds the performance of the Group 1 (10.10%) and Group 2 (10.33%) NSRI portfolios and that of Group 3 (6.39%) (see Hypothesis I). The portfolio performance is also well above the performance of the STOXX Europe 600 Equal Weight NR Index. A further perspective is provided by the Sharpe and Sortino ratios (calculated with monthly data). For each year, the Sharpe ratio shows better risk-adjusted performance (see Table 3.15 and Fig. 3.4).

Table 3.15 Volatility and Sharpe Ratio of the ESG Portfolio and the STOXX Europe 600 Equal Weight Net Return Index

	ESG Portfolio	STOXX Europe 600 Equal Weight NR Index
2Y Volatility	9.93%	8.83%
2Y Sharpe ratio	1.76	1.36
5Y Volatility	10.37%	11.73%
5Y Sharpe ratio	1.55	0.92
10Y Volatility	14.01%	15.50%
10Y Sharpe ratio	0.85	0.48

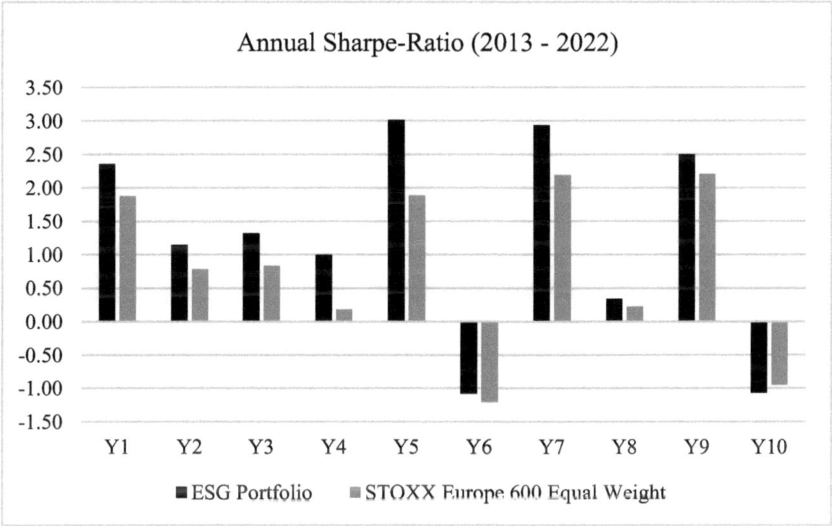

Fig. 3.4 Annual Sharpe Ratio for the ESG Portfolio and the STOXX Europe 600 Equal Weight Net Return Index in 2013–2022. (Note: Own illustration)

With the Sortino ratio, the downside risk is specifically considered, providing a more nuanced evaluation of the portfolio's risk relative to its return. The Sortino ratio also exhibits better downside-adjusted returns over the three periods shown in Table 3.16 compared to the STOXX Europe 600 Equal Weight NR Index. Along with strong outperformance, the Sharpe and Sortino ratios also show better risk-adjusted performance.

Table 3.16 Sortino Ratio of the ESG Portfolio and the STOXX Europe 600 Equal Weight Net Return Index

	ESG Portfolio	STOXX Europe 600 Equal Weight Index
2Y Sortino ratio	4.28	2.84
5Y Sortino ratio	3.05	1.51
10Y Sortino ratio	1.20	0.70

4 Summary and Implementable Model for Practical Applications

In Chap. 2 of this dissertation, it became evident that there is no consensus definition of ESG investing, and this fact is underscored by the diversity of ESG investors. Consequently, the statement that ESG investing comes at the cost of returns is refutable.

The study has also found that ESG ratings and scores may provide an indication of the firm's ESG performance and refer to many ESG indicators. However, they fail to gauge risks in terms of materiality, likelihood of occurrence, and ensuing financial impact (see Sect. 2.3).

The incorporation of sectorally significant ESG factors into investment decision-making contributes to taking into account both substantial risks and opportunities. The analysis in Chap. 3 presented in this dissertation confirmed that sector-relevant ESG metrics serve as proxies for sectoral risk and indicators of companies' governance practices. ESG characteristics and a company's operative success are not disparate factors, as the ESG characteristics reflect a company's operational risk and opportunities and, thus, its financial performance. When these risks are effectively priced into the financial market, capital naturally flows toward companies with robust ESG practices, incentivizing responsible corporate behavior. By allowing investors to integrate ESG metrics into their investment decisions, effective risk pricing can reduce the need for additional regulation and address risk exposure with greater precision than broad regulatory measures.

Furthermore, ESG elements, particularly those related to governance, have long been integral components of investment analysis. Environmental risks and dependencies have been part of company risk assessments. Regulations have resulted in these factors becoming more transparent, clear, and reliable.

A. Schleipfer, *The Value of ESG Metrics in the Investment Process*,
https://doi.org/10.1007/978-3-658-49789-7_4

The findings of this research are effectively captured in the ESG-F model (Fig. 4.1). This model serves as a comprehensive framework for ESG investors, where ESG risks are minimized and opportunities are assessed. The ESG-F model can be used to consider these attributes and benchmarks in detail, a task facilitated by the data reported in this study. With the implementation of the European reporting standards, data quality and availability are expected to improve significantly each year, thereby enhancing the model's precision and reliability in guiding investment decisions.

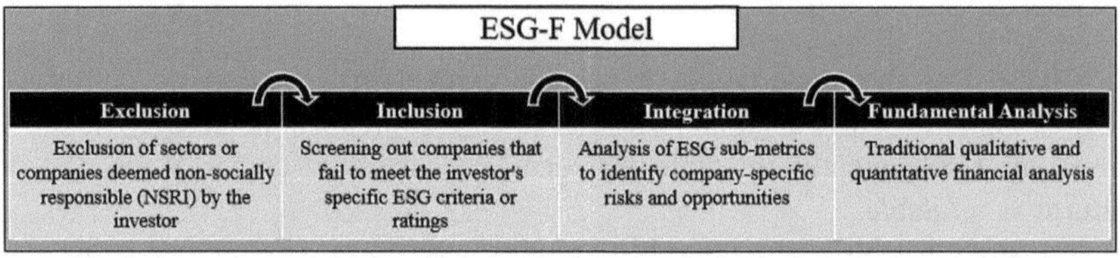

Fig. 4.1 Proposed ESG-F Model. (Note: Own illustration)

The ESG-F model serves as a screening tool for investors who have selected specific sectors or companies for potential investment. With each phase, companies are systematically eliminated from the investment universe, refining the selection until the investor undertakes a more time-consuming, in-depth analysis of the remaining companies in the final phase.

4.1 Exclusion Phase

The ESG investor initiates the analysis with the Exclusion Phase, which involves eliminating companies or sectors deemed incompatible with the investor's ethical standards. This phase may include the exclusion of companies operating in what are considered NSRI sectors, such as tobacco, weapons manufacturing, or fossil fuels. Additionally, an ESG investor may apply further exclusion criteria to remove companies based on their business activities or sector alignment with ESG principles, reflecting broader investor expectations (see Sect. 2.1.3).

From a performance perspective, this dissertation has shown that NSRI companies outperformed the benchmark (see Hypothesis I, Sect. 3.2). These sectors are often, but not always, ignored by ESG fund managers, which might be due to the expectations of investors in ESG funds (see Sect. 2.1.3).

4.2 Inclusion Phase

The Inclusion Phase is a stage during which the investor sets individual ESG thresholds. Often, these reflect specific ESG rating thresholds that summarize the company's general ESG profile. This phase requires an investor's awareness of sector biases, potential methodological changes, and further characteristics discussed in Sect. 2.3.4. Hence, the recommendation is that if ESG ratings are employed, the set threshold should not be excessively high. Companies with an elevated risk profile and potentially weak opportunity profile should be eliminated.

The elimination of companies implicated in ESG controversies, as elaborated in Hypothesis II (see Sect. 3.3) is recommended. This research has shown that companies involved in controversies underperform relative to the benchmark. Hypothesis II has also shown that these controversies cover the 10 UN Global Compact Principles.

4.3 Integration Phase

The integration phase involves detailed assessment of relevant ESG metrics to evaluate company-specific risks and opportunities. Here, the investor should undertake a comprehensive analysis of the relevant ESG factors that could impact long-term financial performance. This could follow the approach used in this dissertation, which includes identifying ESG opportunities and risks relevant to the sector and making use of ESG metrics or simply using the reported findings. Other sources are industry reports and trends, such as from the Global Reporting Initiative or the Sustainability Accounting Standards Board, which provide valuable insights into sectoral ESG issues and opportunities. Another possibility is a scenario analysis, where the investor evaluates how companies might fare in future scenarios of extreme ESG conditions, such as new regulatory laws and increased environmental or societal change.[1] The assessment should be based on ESG KPIs, identifying and quantifying risks and opportunities. Poorly performing companies should be excluded from the investment universe. Hypothesis III

[1] Opportunities are also considered and can be defined with reference to the sources mentioned. An ESG investor, especially a powerful asset manager, has opportunities in transformation-intensive sectors with high transitory and/or physical risks. Transformations, for example to lower CO_2 emissions, change a company's risk profile and thus its valuation.

confirms that metrics serve as reliable proxies for assessing risks and opportunities, providing ESG investors with essential tools for evaluating a company's sustainability and financial potential.

4.4 Fundamental Phase

Finally, the investor focuses on the financial side of the remaining investment options and performs a comprehensive evaluation of each company's fundamentals. By this stage, the investment universe has been refined to include companies that meet the investor's ESG criteria and demonstrate strong financial fundamentals.

References

Abate, G., Basile, I., & Ferrari, P. (2021). The level of sustainability and mutual fund performance in Europe: An empirical analysis using ESG ratings. *Corporate Social Responsibility and Environmental Management*, *28*(5), 1446–1455. https://doi.org/10.1002/csr.2175

Adams, R. J., Smart, P., & Huff, A. S. (2017). Shades of grey: Guidelines for working with the grey literature in systematic reviews for management and organizational studies. *International Journal of Management Reviews*, *19*(4), 432–454. https://doi.org/10.1111/ijmr.12102

Allevi, E., Basso, A., Bonenti, F., Oggioni, G., & Riccardi, R. (2019). Measuring the environmental performance of green SRI funds: A DEA approach. *Energy Economics*, *79*, 32–44. https://doi.org/10.1016/j.eneco.2018.07.023

Amon, J., Rammerstorfer, M., & Weinmayer, K. (2021). Passive ESG portfolio management—The benchmark strategy for socially responsible investors. *Sustainability*, *13*(16), 9388. https://doi.org/10.3390/su13169388

Atz, U., Holt, T. van, Liu, Z. Z., & Bruno, C. (2022). Do corporate sustainability and sustainable finance generate better financial performance? A review and meta-analysis and propositions. *Journal of Sustainable Finance & Investment, Taylor & Francis Journals*, *13*(1), 802–825. https://doi.org/10.1080/20430795.2022.2106934

Baas, J., Schotten, M., Plume, A., Côté, G., & Karimi, R. (2020). Scopus as a curated, high-quality bibliometric data source for academic research in quantitative science studies. *Quantitative Science Studies*, *1*(1), 377–386. https://doi.org/10.1162/qss_a_00019

BCG. (2023). *Global asset management 2023* (21st ed). Retrieved October 23, 2024, from https://web-assets.bcg.com/c8/97/bc0329a046f89c7faeef9ab6a877/bcg-global-asset-management-2023-may-2023.pdf

Beecher, H. K. (1955). The powerful placebo. *Journal of the American Medical Association*, *159*(17), 1602–1606. https://doi.org/10.1001/jama.1955.02960340022006

Berg, F., Kölbel, J., F., & Rigobon, R. (2019). Aggregate confusion: The divergence of ESG ratings. *Forthcoming Review of Finance*. https://doi.org/10.2139/ssrn.3438533

Binnie, I. (2023, June 26). BlackRock's Fink says he's stopped using 'weaponised' term ESG. *Reuters*. Retrieved October 23, 2024, from https://www.reuters.com/business/environment/blackrocks-fink-says-hes-stopped-using-weaponised-term-esg-2023-06-26/

A. Schleipfer, *The Value of ESG Metrics in the Investment Process*,
https://doi.org/10.1007/978-3-658-49789-7

Bioy, H., Stankiewicz, A., Wang, B., Pucci, N., Roy, M., Popat, S., Beaudoin, H. (2024, January 25). *Global sustainable fund flows: Q4 2023 in review*. Morningstar Manager Research Services. Retrieved October 23, 2024, from https://assets.contentstack.io/v3/assets/blt4eb669caa7dc65b2/bltea603fae74386da2/65b7fb3793cdf11bcb7cac4c/Global_ESG_Q4_2023_Flow_Report_final_KG3.pdf

BlackRock. (2024a). *iShares ESG aware MSCI EAFE ETF*. Retrieved October 23, 2024, from https://www.ishares.com/ch/professionals/en/products/283778/ishares-msci-eafe-esg-optimized-etf-f_1?switchLocale=Y

BlackRock. (2024b). Fact sheet iShares Dow Jones Eurozone sustainability screened UCITS ETF (DE). Retrieved October 23, 2024, from https://api.fundinfo.com/document/1e4ea2518d29518b29df09a7097f7206_403867/MR_DE_en_DE000A0F5UG3_YES_2024-09-30.pdf

Bloomberg LP. (n.d.). *ESG and sustainable finance data*. Retrieved October 23, 2024, from https://data.bloomberglp.com/professional/sites/10/389674_CDS_REF_ESG_SFCT_DIG.pdf

Bloomfield, T., Leftwich, R., & Long, J. B. (1977). Portfolio strategies and performance. Journal of Financial Economics, 5(2), 201–218. https://doi.org/10.1016/0304-405X(77)90018-6

Broadhurst, D., Watson, J., & Marshall, J. (Eds.) (2003). *Ethical and socially responsible investment. A reference guide for researchers*. K.G. Saur.

Brodmann, J., Wuthisatian, P., & Malladi, R. K. (2023). The liquidity, performance and investor preference of socially responsible investments. *Review of Behavioral Finance, 15*(2), 224–239. https://doi.org/10.1108/RBF-09-2021-0191

Brush, S. (2022, October 5). BlackRock (BLK) faces more ESG fallout as Louisiana pulls $794 million. *Bloomberg*. Retrieved October 23, 2024, from https://www.bloomberg.com/news/articles/2022-10-05/blackrock-faces-more-esg-fallout-as-louisiana-pulls-794-million

Cerulli Associates & Russell Investments. (2021). *10x10 Report: 3-part series*. Retrieved October 23, 2024, from https://russellinvestments.com/-/media/files/_request/ca/na-cani/10x10-report-3-part-series.pdf

Chandler, J., & Hopewell, S. (2013). Cochrane methods—Twenty years experience in developing systematic review methods. *Systematic Reviews*, *2*, 76, 1–6. https://doi.org/10.1186/2046-4053-2-76

Chomsky, N. (1993). Rethinking Camelot. JFK, the Vietnam War, and US political culture. Haymarket Books.

Christian History Institute. (2024). Wesley's sermon reprints: The use of money. *Christian History Magazine*. Retrieved October 23, 2024, from https://christianhistoryinstitute.org/magazine/article/wesleys-sermon-use-of-money

Cicchetti, D. V. (1994). Guidelines, criteria, and rules of thumb for evaluating normed and standardized assessment instruments in psychology. *Psychological Assessment,* 6(4), 284–290. https://doi.org/10.1037/1040-3590.6.4.284

Clark, H., & Bogran, A. (1999). Foreign direct investment in South Africa. *Denver Journal of International Law & Policy*, *27* (3), 337–358. Retrieved October 23, 2024, from https://digitalcommons.du.edu/djilp/vol27/iss3/2

Cochrane Library. (2023). *About the Cochrane Library*. Retrieved October 23, 2024, from https://www.cochranelibrary.com/about/about-cochrane-library

Collison, D. J., Cobb, G., Power, D. M., & Stevenson, L. A. (2008). The financial performance of the FTSE4Good indices. *Corporate Social Responsibility and Environmental Management, 15*(1), 14–28. https://doi.org/10.1002/csr.144

Cortez, M. C., Silva, F., & Areal, N. (2009). The performance of European socially responsible funds. *Journal of Business Ethics*, 87(4), 573–588. https://doi.org/10.1007/s10551-008-9959-x

Credit Suisse Group AG. (2023). *Sustainable investment framework*. Credit Suisse Group. Retrieved October 23, 2024, from https://www.credit-suisse.com/media/assets/microsite/docs/responsibleinvesting/sustainable-investment-framework.pdf

Cunha, F. A. F. D. S., Oliveira, E. M. de, Orsato, R. J., Klotzle, M. C., Cyrino Oliveira, F. L., & Caiado, R. G. G. (2020). Can sustainable investments outperform traditional benchmarks? Evidence from global stock markets. *Business Strategy and the Environment, 29*(2), 682–697. https://doi.org/10.1002/bse.2397

Davies, H. T., & Crombie, I. K. (1998). Getting to grips with systematic reviews and meta-analyses. *Hospital Medicine, 59*(12), 955–958.

Deloitte. (2023). *Financing the green energy transition: A US$50 trillion catch*. Retrieved October 23, 2024, from https://www2.deloitte.com/content/dam/Deloitte/global/Documents/deloitte-financing-the-green-energy-transition-report-2023.pdf

DeMiguel, V., Garlappi, L., & Uppal, R. (2009). Optimal versus naive diversification: How inefficient is the 1/N portfolio strategy? The Review of Financial Studies, 22(5), 1915–1953. https://doi.org/10.1093/rfs/hhm075

Deutsche Bank AG. (2024). *What is ESG investing?* Retrieved October 23, 2024, from https://www.deutschewealth.com/en/our capabilities/esg/what-is-esg-investing-wealth-management.html

Deutsche Boerse Group. (2024). STOXX® Index methodology guide (portfolio based indices). *Deutsche Boerse*. Retrieved October 23, 2024, from https://www.stoxx.com/document/Indices/Common/Indexguide/stoxx_index_guide.pdf

Diltz, D. J. (1995). The private cost of socially responsible investing. *Applied Financial Economics, 5*(2), 69–77. https://doi.org/10.1080/758529174

Dimson, E., Marsh, P., & Staunton, M. (2020). Divergent ESG ratings. *Journal of Portfolio Management, 47*(1), 75–87. https://doi.org/10.3905/jpm.2020.1.175

Domini, A. L., & Kinder, P. D. (1984). *Ethical investing*. Addison-Wesley.

Donath, L. E., Ioan, R., & Mandimutsira, T. (2018). Evaluating the performance of socially responsible investment funds. *Scientific Annals of Economics and Business, 65*(2), 139–158. https://doi.org/10.2478/saeb-2018-0008

Dorn, M. (2023, May 17). The (Re)balancing act of the S&P 500 ESG Index. *Indexology® Blog*. Retrieved October 23, 2024, from https://www.indexologyblog.com/2022/05/17/the-rebalancing-act-of-the-sp-500-esg-index/

Dornbusch, R., Fischer, S., & Startz, R. (2018). *Macroeconomics* (13th ed). McGraw-Hill Education.

Dreyer, J. K., Moreira, M., Smith, W. T., & Sharma, V. (2023). Do environmental, social and governance practices affect portfolio returns? Evidence from the US stock market from 2002 to 2020. *Review of Accounting and Finance, 22*(1), 37–61. Retrieved October 23, 2024, from https://ideas.repec.org/a/eme/rafpps/raf-02-2022-0046.html

Drucker, P. F. (1993). *The Post-Capitalist Society*. Butterworth-Heinemann.

Dumitrescu, A., Järvinen, J., & Zakriya, M. (2023). Hidden gem or fool's gold: Can passive ESG ETFs outperform the benchmarks? *International Review of Financial Analysis, 86*, 102540. https://doi.org/10.1016/j.irfa.2023.102540

EFRAG. (2023a, December 22). *Publication of the 3 draft EFRAG ESRS IG documents (EFRAG IG 1 TO 3).* Retrieved October 23, 2024, *from* https://www.efrag.org/en/news-and-calendar/news/publication-of-the-3-draft-efrag-esrs-ig-documents-efrag-ig-1-to-3

EFRAG. (2023b, December 23). *Draft EFRAG IG 3 list of ESRS data points.* Retrieved October 23, 2024, from https://efrag.sharefile.com/share/view/s1a12c193b86d406e90b1bcd7b6bb8f6f/fo37c90b-9d9b-4432-a76b-27760cfcc01b

El Ghoul, S., Karoui, A., Patel, S., & Ramani, S. (2023). The green and brown performances of mutual fund portfolios. *Journal of Cleaner Production, 384*, 135267. https://doi.org/10.1016/j.jclepro.2022.135267

ESG Book. (2022, May 5). *ESG Book rebrands as it scales to become the global leader in sustainability data and technology. PR Newswire.* Retrieved October 23, 2024, from https://www.prnewswire.com/news-releases/esg-book-rebrands-as-it-scales-to-become-the-global-leader-in-sustainability-data-and-technology-301554493.html

ESG Book. (2023). *Introduction, Methodology, and FAQs.* Retrieved October 23, 2024, from https://www.esgbook.com/docs/marketing/glass_lewis/GlassLewis_Intro_FAQs.pdf

European Commission. (2018, March 22). *Keynote speech by President Jean-Claude Juncker at the High-Level Conference on Financing Sustainable Growth.* Retrieved October 23, 2024, from https://ec.europa.eu/commission/presscorner/detail/en/SPEECH_18_2402

European Council. (2024, April 29). *Council adopts directive to delay reporting obligations for certain sectors and third country companies.* Retrieved October 23, 2024, from https://www.consilium.europa.eu/en/press/press-releases/2024/04/29/council-adopts-directive-to-delay-reporting-obligations-for-certain-sectors-and-third-country-companies

European Financial Reporting Advisory Group. (2023). *The first set of ESRS – the journey from PTF to delegated act (adopted on 31 July 2023).* Retrieved October 23, 2024, from https://efrag-website.azurewebsites.net/lab6?AspxAutoDetectCookieSupport=1

European Fund and Asset Management Association. (2022). *Asset management report 2022. An overview of the asset management industry.* Retrieved October 23, 2024, *from* https://www.efama.org/sites/default/files/files/Asset%20Management%20Report%202022.pdf

European Parliament. (2024). European Parliament legislative resolution of 24 April 2024 on the proposal for a regulation of the European Parliament and of the Council on the transparency and integrity of Environmental, Social and Governance (ESG) rating activities (COM(2023)0314 – C9-0203/2023 – 2023/0177(COD)). Retrieved October 23, 2024, from https://www.europarl.europa.eu/RegData/seance_pleniere/textes_adoptes/definitif/2024/04-24/0347/P9_TA(2024)0347_EN.pdf

European Parliament & Council of the European Union. (2019). Regulation (EU) 2019/2088 of the European Parliament and of the Council of 27 November 2019 on sustainability-related disclosures in the financial services sector. Retrieved October 23, 2024, from https://eur-lex.europa.eu/eli/reg/2019/2088/oj

Eurosif. (2018). *European SRI Study.* Retrieved October 23, 2024, from https://www.eurosif.org/wp-content/uploads/2021/10/European-SRI-2018-Study.pdf

Eurosif. (2023). *Responsible investment strategies.* Retrieved October 23, 2024, from https://www.eurosif.org/responsible-investment-strategies

Evening Standard. (2023, August 29). *Refinitiv to be scrapped in fresh LSEG rebrand.* Retrieved October 23, 2024, from https://www.standard.co.uk/business/refinitiv-to-be-scrapped-in-fresh-lseg-rebrand-london-stock-exchange-b1103471.html

Ferris, S. P., & Rykaczewski, K. P. (1986). Social investing and portfolio management. Business & Society, 25(1), 1–7. https://doi.org/10.1177/000765038602500101

Financial Stability Board. (2023). *Global monitoring report on non-bank financial intermediation.* Retrieved October 23, 2024, from https://www.fsb.org/wp-content/uploads/P181223.pdf

Fink, A. (2014). *Conducting research literature reviews. From the internet to paper* (4th ed). SAGE.

Fink, L. (2021). Larry Fink's CEO letter 2021. *BlackRock.* Retrieved October 23, 2024, from https://www.blackrock.com/corporate/investor-relations/2021-larry-fink-ceo-letter, updated on 3/28/2024

Foster, L. (2023, March 3). The three letters missing from BlackRock's letter: ESG. *Barrons.* Retrieved October 23, 2024, from https://www.barrons.com/amp/articles/blackrock-letter-esg-b004a3cd

Galema, R., Plantinga, A., & Scholtens, B. (2008). The stocks at stake: Return and risk in socially responsible investment. *Journal of Banking & Finance, 32*(12), 2646–2654. https://doi.org/10.1016/j.jbankfin.2008.06.002

Gernsheimer, O., Kanbach, D. K., & Gast, J. (2021). Coopetition research – A systematic literature review on recent accomplishments and trajectories. *Industrial Marketing Management, 96*, 113–134. https://doi.org/10.1016/j.indmarman.2021.05.001

Ghoul, S. E., & Karoui, A. (2022). Fund performance and social responsibility: New evidence using social active share and social tracking error. *Journal of Banking & Finance, 143*, 106598. https://doi.org/10.1016/j.jbankfin.2022.106598

Global Sustainable Investment Alliance. (2020). Global sustainable investment review 2020. GSIA.

Global Sustainable Investment Alliance. (2023). *Global Sustainable Investment Review 2022.* GSIA. Retrieved October 23, 2024, from https://www.gsi-alliance.org/wp-content/uploads/2023/12/GSIA-Report-2022.pdf

Harzing, A. W., & Alakangas, S. (2016). Google Scholar, Scopus and the Web of Science: A longitudinal and cross-disciplinary comparison. *Scientometrics, 106*(2), 787–804. https://doi.org/10.1007/s11192-015-1798-9

Heinkel, R., Kraus, A., & Zechner, J. (2001). The effect of green investment on corporate behavior. *The Journal of Financial and Quantitative Analysis, 36*(4), 431–449. https://doi.org/10.2307/2676219

Higgins, J. P. T. (2020). *Cochrane handbook for systematic reviews of interventions* (2nd ed). Wiley-Blackwell. Retrieved October 23, 2024, from https://livivo.idm.oclc.org/login?url=https://ebookcentral.proquest.com/lib/zbmed-ebooks/detail.action?docID=5906330

Huang, M. Y., Rojas, R. R., & Convery, P. D. (2020). Forecasting stock market movements using Google Trend searches. *Empirical Economics, 59*(6), 2821–2839. https://doi.org/10.1007/s00181-019-01725-1

Insurance Europe. (2021). *Statistics. 5 key facts about the European insurance industry.* Retrieved October 23, 2024, from https://www.insuranceeurope.eu/statistics

International Financial Reporting Standards Foundation. (2023). *IFRS S2 climate-related disclosures, 2023.* Retrieved October 23, 2024, from https://www.ifrs.org/issued-standards/ifrs-sustainability-standards-navigator/ifrs-s2-climate-related-disclosures.html/content/dam/ifrs/publications/html-standards-issb/english/2023/issued/issbs2

International Monetary Fund. (2024). *World economic outlook database*. Retrieved October 23, 2024, from https://www.imf.org/en/Publications/WEO/weo-database/2023/April, updated on 3/28/2024

ISS ESG (2023). *ISS ESG Corporate Rating*. Retrieved October 23, 2024, from https://www.issgovernance.com/esg/ratings/corporate-rating/

JustETF. (2023). *Largest ETFs in Europe by Rating Provider and Assets Under Management* [Data compiled from various pages]. Retrieved October 23, 2024, from https://www.justetf.com

Kaempfer, W. H., Lehman, J. A., & Lowenberg, A. D. (1987). Divestment, investment sanctions, and disinvestment: An evaluation of anti-apartheid policy instruments. *International Organization, 41*(3), 457–473. https://doi.org/10.1017/S0020818300027545

Kerber, R. (2022, December 1). Florida pulls $2 bln from BlackRock in largest anti-ESG divestment. *Reuters*. Retrieved October 23, 2024, from https://www.reuters.com/business/finance/florida-pulls-2-bln-blackrock-largest-anti-esg-divestment-2022-12-01

Kerber, R., & and Jin, H. (2022, May 19). Tesla cut from S&P 500 ESG Index, and Elon Musk tweets his fury. *Reuters*. Retrieved October 23, 2024, from https://www.reuters.com/business/sustainable-business/tesla-removed-sp-500-esg-index-autopilot-discrimination-concerns-2022-05-18/

Khan, K. S., Kunz, R., Kleijnen, J., & Antes, G. (2003). Five steps to conducting a systematic review. *Journal of the Royal Society of Medicine, 96*(3), 118–121. https://doi.org/10.1258/jrsm.96.3.118

Knight, R. (1990). Sanctions, disinvestments and US corporations in South Africa. In R. R. Edgar (Ed.), *Sanctioning apartheid. Africa World Press, Inc.,* 67–89. Retrieved October 23, 2024, from https://africanactivist.msu.edu/recordFiles/210-849-25021/32-130-24E-84-african_activist_archive-a0a9b8-b_12419.pdf

Knudsen, J. S. (2011). Company delistings from the UN Global Compact: Limited business demand or domestic governance failure? *Journal of Business Ethics, 103*(3), 331–349. https://doi.org/10.1007/s10551-011-0875-0

Koo, Terry K., & Li, Mae Y. (2016). A Guideline of Selecting and Reporting Intraclass Correlation Coefficients for Reliability Research. *Journal of chiropractic medicine*, 15 (2), pp. 155–163. https://doi.org/10.1016/j.jcm.2016.02.012

Lawson, S., Boskovic, T., Zurowska, E., Shimizu, A., & DeRubeis, D. (2022). After the great resignation – Shifting expectations for employers. *BlackRock*. Retrieved October 23, 2024, from https://www.blackrock.com/cash/literature/whitepaper/after-the-great-resignation-shifting-expectations-for-employers.pdf

Lean, H. H., Ang, W. R., & Smyth, R. (2014). Performance persistence of socially responsible investment funds in the Asia Pacific region. In G. N. Gregoriou, & D. L. K. Chuen (Eds.), *Handbook of Asian finance: REITs, trading and fund performance* (pp. 377–392). Elsevier Academic Press. Retrieved October 23, 2024, from https://www.sciencedirect.com/science/article/pii/B9780128009864000200

Leite, P., & Cortez, M. C. (2015). Performance of European socially responsible funds during market crises: Evidence from France. *International Review of Financial Analysis, 40*, 132–141. https://doi.org/10.1016/j.irfa.2015.05.012

Li, K., Rollins, J., & Yan, E. (2018). Web of Science use in published research and review papers 1997–2017: A selective, dynamic, cross-domain, content-based analysis. *Scientometrics, 115*(1), 1–20. https://doi.org/10.1007/s11192-017-2622-5

Lodh, A. (2020, February 25). ESG and the cost of capital. *MSCI*. Retrieved October 23, 2024, from https://www.msci.com/www/blog-posts/esg-and-the-cost-of-capital/01726513589

Luxembourg for Finance. (2021). *Future challenges for the insurance industry. The largest institutional investor in Europe*. Retrieved October 23, 2024, from https://www.luxembourgforfinance.com/de/publication-article/future-challenges-for-the-insurance-industry-de

Lydenberg, S. (2020, October 6). A brief history of sustainable and impact investment: It's still not too late to save the planet. *Domini*. Retrieved October 23, 2024, from https://domini.com/insights/a-brief-history-of-sustainable-and-impact-investment-its-still-not-too-late-to-save-the-planet

Mankiw, N. G., Romer, D., & Weil, D. N. (1992). A contribution to the empirics of economic growth. *The Quarterly Journal of Economics, 107*(2), 407–437. https://doi.org/10.2307/2118477

Markowitz, G. (2012). The invention of ecocide: Agent Orange, Vietnam, and the scientists who changed the way we think about the environment. By David Zierler. University of Georgia Press, 2011. xii + 245. *Environmental History, 17*(2), 431–433. https://doi.org/10.1093/envhis/ems016

MBDA. (2023). *ASMPA*. Retrieved October 23, 2024, from https://www.mbda-systems.com/product/asmpa/

MBDA. (2024). *About us*. Retrieved October 23, 2024, from https://www.mbda-systems.com/about-us/

Moher, D., Liberati, A., Tetzlaff, J., & Altman, D. G. (2009). Preferred reporting items for systematic reviews and meta-analyses: The PRISMA statement. *PLoS Medicine, 6*(7), e1000097. https://doi.org/10.1371/journal.pmed.1000097

Morgan Stanley Institute for Sustainable Investing. (2019). Sustainable signals. Individual investor interest driven by impact, conviction and choice. *Morgan Stanley*. Retrieved October 23, 2024, from https://www.morganstanley.com/content/dam/msdotcom/infographics/sustainable-investing/Sustainable_Signals_Individual_Investor_White_Paper_Final.pdf

Morgan Stanley Institute for Sustainable Investing. (2024). Sustainable reality. Sustainable funds show continued outperformance and positive flows in 2023 despite a slower second half. *Morgan Stanley*. Retrieved October 23, 2024, from https://www.morganstanley.com/content/dam/msdotcom/en/assets/pdfs/MSInstituteforSustainableInvesting-SustainableRealityFY2023-Final.pdf

Morningstar. (2021). *Morningstar Sustainability Rating Methodology*. Retrieved October 23, 2024, from https://www.morningstar.com/content/dam/marketing/shared/research/methodology/744156_Morningstar_Sustainability_Rating_for_Funds_Methodology.pdf

Morningstar. (2023). *Morningstar's guide to sustainable investing 2023*. Retrieved October 23, 2024, from https://www.brighttalk.com/resource/core/421256/2023-guide-to-sustainable-investing_899221.pdf

Moscowitz, M. (1973, February 11). Why 'good guy' funds have flopped. *The New York Times*. Retrieved October 23, 2024, from https://www.nytimes.com/1973/02/11/archives/why-good-guy-funds-have-flopped.html

MSCI. (2018). *Methodology book*. Retrieved October 23, 2024, from https://www.msci.com/eqb/methodology/meth_docs/MSCI_ESG_Screened_Indexes_Methodology.pdf

MSCI. (2024a). ESG 101: *What is environmental, social and governance?* Retrieved October 23, 2024, from https://www.msci.com/our-solutions/esg-investing/principles-of-sustainable-investing

MSCI. (2024b). *ESG Ratings Methodology.* Retrieved October 23, 2024, from https://www.msci.com/documents/1296102/34424357/MSCI+ESG+Ratings+Methodology.pdf

Muka, T., Glisic, M., Milic, J., Verhoog, S., Bohlius, J., Bramer, W., Chowdhury, R., & Oscar, H. F. (2020). A 24-step guide on how to design, conduct, and successfully publish a systematic review and meta-analysis in medical research. *European Journal of Epidemiology, 35*(1), 49–60. https://doi.org/10.1007/s10654-019-00576-5

Napoletano, E., & Katzeff, P. (2024, January 2). Environmental, social and governance: What is ESG investing? *Forbes*. Retrieved October 23, 2024, from https://www.forbes.com/advisor/investing/esg-investing/

Newman, M., & Gough, D. (2020). Systematic reviews in educational research: Methodology, perspectives and application. In O. Zawacki-Richter, M. Kerres, S. Bedenlier, M. Bond, & K. Buntins (Eds.), *Systematic reviews in educational research. Methodology, perspectives and application* (1st ed). Springer Fachmedien Wiesbaden, 3–22. https://link.springer.com/chapter/https://doi.org/10.1007/978-3-658-27602-7_1

Nguyen, H. L., & Kanbach, D. K. (2023). Toward a view of integrating corporate sustainability into strategy: A systematic literature review. *Corporate Social Responsibility and Environmental Management, 31*(2), 962–976. https://doi.org/10.1002/csr.2611

Ocean Tomo. (2022). *Intangible asset market value study.* Retrieved October 23, 2024, from https://oceantomo.com/intangible-asset-market-value-study/

Opimas. (2022, June 16). ESG data market could exceed $1.3bn in 2022. *Environment Analyst*. Retrieved October 23, 2024, from https://environment-analyst.com/global/108032/esg-data-market-could-exceed-13bn-in-2022

Opimas. (2023). *ESG data is now worth it.* Retrieved October 23, 2024, from https://www.opimas.com/research/742/detail/, updated on 5/16/2023

Opimas. (2024). *The market for ESG data in 2024.* Retrieved October 23, 2024, from https://www.opimas.com/research/982/detail/

Paul, J., Lim, W. M., O'Cass, A., Hao, A. W., & Bresciani, S. (2021). Scientific procedures and rationales for systematic literature reviews (SPAR-4-SLR). *International Journal of Consumer Studies, 45*(4), O1–O16. https://doi.org/10.1111/ijcs.12695

Pav, S. E. (2021). *The Sharpe ratio. Statistics and applications.* Chapman & Hall (CRC).

Penedones, A., Alves, C., & Batel-Marques, F. (2019). Recommendations to conduct and report systematic reviews in medical literature: A scoping review. *BMC Medical Research Methodology, 19*(1), 234. https://doi.org/10.1186/s12874-019-0870-1

Priem, R., & Gabellone, A. (2022). The impact of a firm's ESG score on its cost of capital: Can a high ESG score serve as a substitute for a weaker legal environment? https://doi.org/10.2139/ssrn.4286057

Prol, J. L., & Kim, K. (2022). Risk-return performance of optimized ESG equity portfolios in the NYSE. *Finance Research Letters, 50*, 103312. https://doi.org/10.1016/j.frl.2022.103312

Rahman, S., Lee, C. F., & Xiao, Y. (2017). The investment performance, attributes, and investment behavior of ethical equity mutual funds in the US: An empirical investigation. *Review of Quantitative Finance and Accounting, 49*(1), 91–116. https://doi.org/10.1007/s11156-016-0581-1

Rasche, A., Gwozdz, W., Lund-Larsen, M., & Moon, J. (2018). Which firms leave MSIs? A resource dependence perspective on the UN Global Compact. *Proceedings, 2018*(1), 10459. https://doi.org/10.5465/AMBPP.2018.10459abstract

Refinitiv Eikon. (2022). *Refinitiv ESG scores.* Retrieved October 23, 2024, from https://www.refinitiv.com/content/dam/marketing/en_us/documents/fact-sheets/esg-scores-fact-sheet.pdf

Renneboog, L., Ter Horst, J., & Zhang, C. (2008a). Socially responsible investments: Institutional aspects, performance, and investor behavior. *Journal of Banking & Finance, 32*(9), 1723–1742. https://doi.org/10.1016/j.jbankfin.2007.12.039

Renneboog, L., Ter Horst, J., & Zhang, C. (2008b). The price of ethics and stakeholder governance: The performance of socially responsible mutual funds. *Journal of Corporate Finance, 14*(3), 302–322. https://doi.org/10.1016/j.jcorpfin.2008.03.009

Revelli, C., & Viviani, J. L. (2015). Financial performance of socially responsible investing (SRI): What have we learned? A meta-analysis. *Business Ethics, the Environment & Responsibility, 24*(2), 158–185. https://doi.org/10.1111/beer.12076

Richardson, B. J., & Cragg, W. (2010). Being virtuous and prosperous: SRI's conflicting goals. *Journal of Business Ethics, 92*(S1), 21–39. https://doi.org/10.1007/s10551-010-0632-9

S&P Global. (2022). *S&P Global ESG Scores – Methodology.* Retrieved October 23, 2024, from https://www.spglobal.com/esg/documents/sp-global-esg-scores-methodology-2022.pdf

S&P Global. (2024). *ESG Scores and Raw Data.* Retrieved October 23, 2024, from https://www.spglobal.com/esg/solutions/esg-scores-data

Schueth, S. (2003). Socially responsible investing in the United States. *Journal of Business Ethics, 43*(3), 189–194. https://doi.org/10.1023/A:1022981828869

Schulmerich, M., Leporcher, Y. M., & Eu, C. H. (2015). *Applied asset and risk management. A guide to modern portfolio management and behavior-driven markets* (1st ed). Springer.

Shrout, P. E., & Fleiss, J. L. (1979). Intraclass correlations: Uses in assessing rater reliability. *Psychological Bulletin, 86*(2), 420–428. https://doi.org/10.1037//0033-2909.86.2.420

Simon, J. G., Powers, C. W., & Gunnemann, J. P. (1972). The ethical investor. Universities and corporate responsibility. New Haven: Yale University Press. https://doi.org/10.1177/000271627441100192

Sparkes, R. (2002). *Socially responsible investment. A global revolution.* Wiley.

State Street Global Advisors. (2024, April). *Fact sheet: State Street World ESG Index Equity Fund.* Retrieved October 23, 2024, from https://www.ssga.com/library-content/products/factsheets/mf/emea/factsheet-emea-en_gb-lu1159235362.pdf

Steen, M., Moussawi, J. T., & Gjolberg, O. (2020). Is there a relationship between Morningstar's ESG ratings and mutual fund performance? *Journal of Sustainable Finance & Investment, 10*(4), 349–370. https://doi.org/10.1080/20430795.2019.1700065

Stellman, J. M., Stellman, S. D., Christian, R., Weber, T., & Tomasallo, C. (2003). The extent and patterns of usage of Agent Orange and other herbicides in Vietnam. *Nature, 422*(6933), 681–687. https://doi.org/10.1038/nature01537

Stewart, J. B. (2011). Amandla! The Sullivan Principles and the battle to end apartheid in South Africa, 1975–1987. *The Journal of African American History, 96*(1), 62–89. https://doi.org/10.5323/jafriamerhist.96.1.0062

Subrata, R. (2017). SRI investment & screening performance: An empirical study. *Pacific Business Review International, 9*(11), 30–41. Retrieved October 23, 2024, from http://www.pbr.co.in/2017/2017_month/May/04.pdf

SustainAbility. (2020). *Rate the raters 2020 report*. Retrieved October 23, 2024, from https://www.sustainability.com/globalassets/sustainability.com/thinking/pdfs/sustainability-ratetheraters2020-report.pdf

Sustainalytics. (2020). *Overview of Sustainalytics' ESG Risk Ratings*. Retrieved October 23, 2024, from https://connect.sustainalytics.com/hubfs/SFS/Sustainalytics%20ESG%20Risk%20Ratings_Issuer%20Backgrounder.pdf

Tanner-Smith, E. E., Egger, M., & Higgins, J. (2019). Systematic reviews in health research. *Research Synthesis Methods, 10*(3), 310–311. https://doi.org/10.1002/jrsm.1376

Tranfield, D., Denyer, D., & Smart, P. (2003). Towards a methodology for developing evidence-informed management knowledge by means of systematic review. *British Journal of Management, 14*(3), 207–222. https://doi.org/10.1111/1467-8551.00375

TCFD. (2017). *Recommendations of the Task Force on Climate-related Financial Disclosures*. Retrieved October 23, 2024, from https://assets.bbhub.io/company/sites/60/2021/10/FINAL-2017-TCFD-Report.pdf

UNEP FI. (n.d.). *Net-Zero Asset Owner Alliance*. Retrieved October 23, 2024, from https://www.unepfi.org/net-zero-alliance/

UNEP FI. (2021). *The Net-Zero Insurance Alliance – Statement of commitment by signatory companies*. Retrieved October 23, 2024, from https://www.unepfi.org/psi/wp-content/uploads/2021/07/NZIA-Commitment.pdf

UNEP FI. (2024a). *Members*. United Nations Environment Programme, Finance Initiative. Retrieved October 23, 2024, from https://www.unepfi.org/net-zero-insurance/members/, updated on 3/29/2024

UNEP FI. (2024b, April 25). *New UN multistakeholder forum to drive progress on the insurance transition to net zero*. United Nations Environment Programme, Finance Initiative. Retrieved October 23, 2024, from https://www.unepfi.org/industries/insurance/new-un-multistakeholder-forum-to-drive-progress-on-the-insurance-transition-to-net-zero/

United Nations Framework Convention on Climate Change. (2023). *Introduction to climate finance*. Retrieved October 23, 2024, from https://unfccc.int/topics/introduction-to-climate-finance

United Nations. (2004). *The Global Compact – Who cares wins – Connecting financial markets to a changing world*. United Nations Global Compact. Retrieved October 23, 2024, from https://www.unglobalcompact.org/docs/issues_doc/Financial_markets/who_cares_who_wins.pdf

United Nations. (2006). *Secretary-General launches 'Principles for Responsible Investment' Backed by World's largest Investors. United Nations Press Release*. Retrieved October 23, 2024, from https://press.un.org/en/2006/sg2111.doc.htm

Wesley, J. (2024). *The sermons of John Wesley: The use of money*. Wesley Center Online. Retrieved October 23, 2024, from http://wesley.nnu.edu/john-wesley/the-sermons-of-john-wesley-1872-edition/sermon-50-the-use-of-money/

Westing, A. H. (1983). The environmental aftermath of warfare in Viet Nam. *Natural Resources Journal, 23*(2), 365–389

Wilkes, T. (2023, June 2). US regulation fears drive insurers' climate alliance break-up. *Reuters*. Retrieved October 23, 2024, from https://www.reuters.com/sustainability/us-regulation-fears-drive-insurers-climate-alliance-break-up-2023-06-01/

Wilkes, T., Hübner, A., & Sims, T. (2023, May 26). Insurers flee climate alliance after ESG backlash in the US. *Reuters*. Retrieved October 23, 2024, from https://www.reuters.com/business/allianz-decides-leave-net-zero-insurance-alliance-2023-05-25/

Woods, I., Sullivan. R., Koshy, A., Merrienboer, R. van, & Slebos, M. (2022). *Review of trends in ESG reporting requirements for investors*. UNPRI. Retrieved October 23, 2024, from https://www.unpri.org/download?ac=16705

Zhang, J., Yu, Q., Zheng, F., Long, C., Lu, Z., & Duan, Z. (2016). Comparing keywords plus of WOS and author keywords: A case study of patient adherence research. *Journal of the Association for Information Science and Technology*, *67*(4), 967–972. https://doi.org/10.1002/asi.23437

Zhu, J., & Liu, W. (2020). A tale of two databases: The use of Web of Science and Scopus in academic papers. *Scientometrics*, *123*(1), 321–335. https://doi.org/10.1007/s11192-020-03387-8

MIX
Papier aus verantwortungsvollen Quellen
Paper from responsible sources
FSC® C105338

If you have any concerns about our products,
you can contact us on
ProductSafety@springernature.com

In case Publisher is established outside the EU,
the EU authorized representative is:
Springer Nature Customer Service Center GmbH
Europaplatz 3, 69115 Heidelberg, Germany

Printed by Libri Plureos GmbH
in Hamburg, Germany